5753

blue
rider
press

MY CUBS

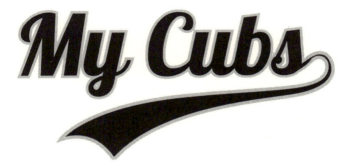

A LOVE STORY

SCOTT SIMON

BLUE RIDER PRESS

NEW YORK

blue
rider
press

An imprint of Penguin Random House LLC
375 Hudson Street
New York, New York 10014

Library of Congress Cataloging-in-Publication Data
Names: Simon, Scott, author.
Title: My Cubs : a love story / Scott Simon.
Description: New York : Blue Rider Press, 2017.
Identifiers: LCCN 2017004698 (print) | LCCN 2017006913 (ebook) | ISBN
9780735218031 (hardback) | ISBN 9780735218048 (EPub)
Subjects: LCSH: Chicago Cubs (Baseball team)—History. | Simon,
Scott—Childhood and youth. | Baseball fans—Illinois—Chicago—Biography.
| Chicago (Ill.)—Biography | BISAC: SPORTS & RECREATION / Baseball /
Essays & Writings. | SPORTS & RECREATION / Baseball / History.
| BIOGRAPHY & AUTOBIOGRAPHY / Sports.
Classification: LCC GV875.C6 S49 2017 (print)
| LCC GV875.C6 (ebook) | DDC 796.357/640977311—dc23
LC record available at https://lccn.loc.gov/2017004698

Printed in the United States of America
1   3   5   7   9   10   8   6   4   2

BOOK DESIGN BY GRETCHEN ACHILLES
INTERIOR ILLUSTRATIONS BY GARY BULLOCK

For Chicago

Thanks for making room for me.

I have this dream. It's the seventh game of the World Series, bottom of the ninth inning, Cubs against the Yankees, and the bases are loaded. The score is 2–1, Cubs, but the Yanks are threatening. (The Yankees haven't been a great team for years, but they're still satisfying to beat in dreams.) Wrigley Field boils and churns with cheers, claps, and fans on their feet waving "W" flags.

The green field glows. The ivy on the walls gleams under the bright white light and rustles in the crisp lake wind.

The Cubs are an out away from winning a World Series, against all odds. But they've run out of pitchers. Fergie Jenkins, Kerry Wood, Jon Lester, Kyle Hendricks, Greg

Maddux, and Mordecai "Three Finger" Brown (an improbable all-era roster of Cubs All-Stars) have all thrown brilliantly. But the bullpen is almost bare. The manager (a gray-haired, knob-nosed fusion of Joe Maddon, Charlie Grimm, and Joe McCarthy) is downcast and flummoxed. Then a light goes on in his eyes.

"It's a crazy idea, I know," he tells his coaches. "But I got a feeling . . ."

I hear my name crackle over the old tin speakers and echo over the slatted green seats and scuffed concrete stairs. Astonishment rolls through the crowd. The announcers (who sound like Joe Buck and Bob Costas) are stupefied, if not quite speechless. "A move no one could have predicted . . ." I take slow, deliberate strides over the electrified green grass and look down to see my arms in white sleeves with Cubby blue stripes.

I reach the mound. Some of the astounded hubbub dies. The catcher (all grit and spit, a grizzled combination of Randy Hundley, Gabby Hartnett, and David Ross) hands me the ball. "No need to go over signs," he says through a chaw and a grin. He knows I have just one pitch: a fat, slow dodo of a throw that catches the wind like a candy wrapper, darts, floats, curves, and is preposterously difficult to hit.

My catcher returns to crouch behind home plate. In the broadcast booth, Joe and Bob sputter to explain this stunning turn. "He's a fan. But he knows a lot about the franchise, and he's been practicing his pitch at the gym. And the Cubs must have seen something they liked, because here he is . . ."

The Yankee batter glowers and spits. He's not Derek, Gehrig, or the Mick, but some malevolent, swearing, gob-spitting, steel-bearded, pinstriped brute. In fact, let's call him the Brute. He tells our catcher, "Look what the cat dragged to the mound." Then the Brute glares at me: "Time for batting practice, rook."

I take a deep breath. The seats at Wrigley roil with 43,000 Cubs fans who take a sudden deep breath at the same time and fall silent. I look to my right to see the All-Star Cubs spirits of Kris Bryant and Ron Santo dance on their toes at third, and Addison Russell, Ernie Banks, and Joe Tinker at short. I glance to my right: Javy Báez and Ryno Sandberg are on patrol at second base, while Anthony Rizzo and Mark Grace spit and pound the pockets of their gloves at first.

I look in to my catcher. I draw back my arms. I twist slightly to put my power into the psoas muscle (as my yoga trainer has taught me) and bring my right arm through above my shoulder, snapping off the throw with my right hand.

All action seems to slow. I see the ball hang in the night air, snag the lake wind, then float and weave, its red seams whirling. The Brute spits, then swings mightily. But the fat of his bat misses by six inches, and I hear—43,000 fans hear—his swing whiff the air like a tree cracking and falling.

"Stee-rike!"

The Brute steps back to spit and swear. He wipes his huge, grimy hands across his pinstripes and yells out to the mound, "Try that again, meat. I got your number now."

My wife, Caroline, our daughters, Elise and Paulina, our dog, and my late mother sit together in grandstand seats along the third base line. All but our dog, Daisy, have their heads lowered in anticipated embarrassment. (Daisy *believes*.) My mother tells all nearby, "Well, you know, darlings, all that writing stuff came later. Pitching for the Cubs is really what he's always wanted to do. I just hope . . ."

I shake off my catcher's sign, but it's an act; I'll throw the same pitch, and hope he won't see it coming. I rear back, thrust forward, and let the ball go from the tips of my fingers. It bobs and weaves as capriciously as the flight of a firefly. The Brute holds back for an instant, addled and confused, then tries to punch the ball with his bat.

The gesture looks desperate and pathetic. The Brute misses by a foot. The roar of the crowd is so loud I can only read the lips of the ump as he bellows, "Stee-rike two!"

Up in the booth, Bob and Joe agree as one. "Nothing quite like this has ever been seen in baseball history. The Chicago Cubs—historically one of the most beloved, but easily the most cursed, hexed, and jinxed franchise in sports history—are a strike away from winning the World Series and have bet it all on a longtime fan with a freakishly effective pitch. How amazing! How utterly . . . Cub-like!"

Ernie Banks trots in from short to hold up a single, slim finger. "Just one more, Scooter, one more!" Ron Santo and Kris Bryant pound their gloves at third, while Javy and Ryno draw their toes around second base. I shake off a first sign. Then a second, then a third. My catcher, who knows this plan, gives his plump brown glove a last thump and holds it over the heart of the plate. I rear back and rock my psoas. But this time, I don't snap off a last floater of a pitch—what the Brute, the NSA, the KGB, MI5, and thousands in the stands and sixty million people tuned in at home expect. Instead, I bring my right arm through with the power of a rocket burst. The seams on the ball whizz and whirr into a blinding blur.

The crowd inhales. The Brute rocks back on his heels, too astonished even to lift his bat from his shoulders.

The radar gun flickers before it glows with three numerals: *101 mph*. My fastball smacks the catcher's mitt like a crack of lightning. The Brute thumps his hitless bat on the ground in defeat and frustration, where it leaves an angry gash the size of a canal. The ump cries, "Strike three!" Joe and Bob sputter, "I can't believe it! I can't believe it! Against all odds, and after more than a century . . ." as Ernie, Ron, Ryno, Kris, Javy, Gabby, David, Fergie, Kyle, Jon, and Kerry pile all over me on the mound and a sea of Cubby blue fills the Friendly Confines of the greatest and greenest old brick ballpark, with her ivy-covered walls.

I am a Cubs fan. A husband and father, an American, a Chicagoan, and a Cubs fan. My politics, religion, and personal tastes change with whatever I learn from life. But being a Cubs fan is my nature, my heritage, and probably somewhere in my chromosomes.

If you prick me, I'm quite sure I'll bleed Cubby blue.

I am in the news business, and try to keep myself apprised of the timeliest information about unrest, wars, finance, and affairs of state. But in the morning, I usually check the scores of Cubs games the moment my feet hit the floor.

I've been blessed to see the Rose City of Petra, the Pink City of Jaipur, and the gracefully gushing fountains in the Place de la Concorde. But I still can't imagine a more beautiful place on earth than Wrigley Field, an ivied spot in a city setting of red brick against lakefront towers, especially on a soft August afternoon or crisp autumn night.

In the poetic opening words of *The Adventures of Augie March*, Saul Bellow defines the churning urban forces that have shaped his title character. I've made a few adjustments:

I am an American, north side Chicago born—Chicago, that City of Big Shoulders—and go at things as I have taught myself, free-style, and will make the record in my own way: first to knock, and historically often dead last in the National League. But a man's character is his fate, says Heraclitus, or as Moe Drabowsky, the Cubs pitcher, once put it, "We came out of the dugout for opening day and saw a fan holding up a sign: 'Wait 'Til Next Year.'"

To be devoted to the Chicago Cubs is to carry a torch of love that defies comparison. If rooting for the New York Yankees has been like rooting for Wal-Mart or Microsoft, what has it been like to root for the Cubs?

No metaphor for doom has ever improved on "rooting for the Chicago Cubs."

People used to use compare the Cubs to the *Hindenburg* and the *Titanic*. But lives were actually lost in those failures; and besides, they sank just once. The Cubs couldn't win a World Series for *108 years*.

During those decades, scientists split the atom in Chicago. Chicagoans built towers that scraped the sky. They improvised a new kind of comedy and transformed drama. Chicago writers pumped blood and muscle into literature. A Chicagoan walked on the moon. Chicagoans won Nobel Prizes in every category and invented Twinkies, *Playboy* magazine, and open-heart surgery. A Chicago man was elected president of the United States. (And actually, I'm glad it was a White Sox fan. A Cubs fan with nuclear weapons? I imagine a mushroom cloud over Milwaukee. "Oh, jeez, I thought that was to call for a pizza . . .")

But the Chicago Cubs still couldn't win the World Series. The Cubs have been the passion that confirms the triumph of hope over experience.

During the holiday season that followed the Cubs 2016 World Series win, a department store Santa Claus caught my eye with a white-gloved wave. He told his elves to let me approach his gilded chair. Santa reached below his throne, doffed his signature red stocking cap, and pulled on a Cubs hat.

"I was a marine," Santa said. "Went to 'Nam in sixty-nine. By August, Cubs were nine games up in the National League race," he continued, "when they sent me out into the *shit*." Santa swore like a sailor, or anyhow like a marine. "No Twitter-twat or e-mail in those days. We couldn't listen to that *Good Morning, Vietnam* guy either, or Charlie would find us. It was just us, Charlie, and the shit. By the time I got out of the jungle, it was December. I grabbed hold of the first guy I saw in the clear and shook him to pieces. 'Who the hell won the World Series?' I asked. 'Who won?' 'Oh, New York,' he told me, and I said, 'Fucking Yankees, again, hey? Well, at least the Cubs finally got our chance.' And this kid says, 'No sir. It was the New York Mets what won.' And I shouted at him, 'The Mets? Fucking Mets, not even the Yanks? The goddamn Cubs had a nine-game lead! Did the team bus run off a cliff? Goddamn mother-loving ass-licking . . .'" Santa Cub grew exhaustively vulgar. "'I survived the *shit* just to hear that the Cubs *blew it* again?'"

"But this year . . ." I told him, and Santa Cub jiggled his post-marine belly like a bowlful of jelly.

"We earned the World Series 108 times over, hey? Our daddies and mammies and grandparents. Me and you."

A few more families had lined up to see him, and Santa switched back to his home-field red headgear. He adjusted his belly like an umpire's chest protector.

"C'mon, kids," he called over to the families. "Step on over and say hello. Just chatting with this nice man. Santa and this man already got our present, didn't we, pallie? One we've waited for a long time."

Santa really does have a twinkle in his eye.

Cubs games were in the air on the north side of Chicago. My grade school was just a block north and five blocks east of Wrigley Field, my high school twenty blocks north, and from mid-April to the end of school, and then again in September until the nip in the air began to bite, sounds from Cubs games would float in through the open windows of our classrooms, like gusts from the lake. Our social studies teacher would scratch something like *bicameral legislature* in white letters across the green board (the colors of the scoreboard at Wrigley Field), and now and then we could hear a faint chorus of gasps or, even more occasionally, cheers.

"Homer?" someone in the back would ask in a whisper.

My last name begins with *S*; I was lucky to usually have a seat in a rear row. Speculative commentary about the game we couldn't see could proceed without interruption.

"Double, maybe."

"Who they playing?"

"Cards. *Gibson*."

"Damn."

The Cubs played only day games then, which usually began at 1:15 in the afternoon. School would get out at 3:15. By the time our El train had passed Thorndale, Bryn Mawr, Berwyn, Argyle, Lawrence, Wilson, and the S curve of Sheridan to pull into the Addison Street platform, we could lift ourselves from our seats to look out the windows to see if they had raised a flag yet (as, of course, they still do) above Wrigley's green and white-lettered scoreboard: "W" for a win, "L" for a loss. We saw a lot of "Ls."

"Damn."

"I told you—they suck."

The word was a little sharper then. It had sexual implications. It rhymed with, and was companion to, the F word. You wouldn't say it in class, or to a parent, without consequences. It was a word you kept all day in your pocket for the ride home on the El to show your pals you knew it—in all its implications. We each took a turn.

"Yeah, suck the big one."

"They suck, but they're getting better."

"Better at sucking."

"Maybe they won't suck tomorrow."

(When word got out in 2016 that Joe Maddon, the Cubs manager, had told his team as the season began, "Just try not to suck," I knew the Cubs had finally found the right man to steer them to a championship.)

We'd ride south, past Belmont, Wellington, Diversey, Fullerton, and Armitage, where the El trains threaded down into the subway tunnels, toward Clark and Division. I'd try to take looks into the open windows of the second floors of the north side territory, where the Cubs were the local favorites. I didn't know of any ten-minute ride on earth that might give you more glimpses of life: flowered curtains flapping in pink and blue bedrooms, ironing boards on struts in yellow-walled kitchens, gray-haired women in printed blouses and children in gray sweatshirts resting their heads on their folded hands along window-sills, men in stained, stiff blue coveralls working over engines, red Chinese characters flickering in lighted signs, white-capped mugs of beer with cool blue mottos, FROM THE LAND OF SKY BLUE WATERS, BREWED IN GOD'S COUNTRY, Greek Orthodox crosses, Stars of David, crucifixes, red, orange, and silver-white neon letters blaring RED-HOTS, WIRE TRANSFERS, PODIATRIST, PALM READER, TACOS, 24-HOUR, TEAMSTERS, OPTOMETRIST, PIZZA-PIZZA-PIZZA, WARD COMMITTEEMAN, CHARRED POLISH, HAPPY HOUR, CHECKS CASHED, BAGELS, BAR-B-Q, LOTTERY TICKETS, DHOSAS, BARBACOA, WASH-DRY-FOLD, ALWAYS OPEN, and CHRIST DIED FOR OUR SINS.

At a time when so many teams were moving into nameless new exurbs and abandoned downtown lots, the Cubs were still the hometown team of a neighborhood that, as far as we could see, held the whole world in a few city blocks. There were better baseball teams for sure. But no better team to root for, in no better place, than the Cubs.

Many afternoons after class in grade school, my friends and I would become mini-Cubs, playing whatever kind of baseball game we could manage in the parking lot of our school. Often, we wouldn't play a two-sided game, but would put as many friends as we could muster onto the field and let each boy take a turn at bat until it was dark. The play, not the score, was important; we were Cubs fans.

Avi, Billy, Bruce, Danny (a White Sox fan), Lewie, Stu, and I would stand up to the plate and waggle our bats and butts in imitation of our favorite players. We'd stand square up, like Ron Santo, to hold the bat almost parallel to our shoulders. Or we'd clench the bat as upright as a light pole, hoping to swing with the elegant lefty fluency of Billy Williams. And all of us tried to tuck the bat just behind our hips, dip into a slight crouch, and drum our fingers on the barrel—deliberately, not impatiently—as we waited for the pitch so we could turn on the ball with our wrists like the spring of a trap, hoping to emulate the swing of Ernie Banks.

I often pitched, and when I did, I'd try to embody the easy, unfussy pitching motion of Ferguson Jenkins. Fergie had grown up in Chatham, Ontario. He told me once that he sharpened his pitching finesse by trying to throw lumps of coal from a nearby rail yard between the gaps of passing boxcars. (I used to try to throw acorns between the slats of green wooden benches in front of bus stops, which is not nearly as interesting.)

Ferguson Jenkins would win twenty games in six consecutive seasons for the Cubs. But he needed a couple of innings to find a rhythm and settle into a game. Fergie often gave up solo home runs in those early innings, and glitches seemed to give him an edge to slice through the rest of the game (and Fergie would lead both leagues in complete games, in four seasons total). So if Billy or Bruce hit a pitch that soared over our heads and rolled under the Broadway bus, I'd play a voice in my head: "The big right-hander needs a few batters to find his rhythm. Then he'll be untouchable . . ."

We performed each at-bat with imagined play-by-play: "Bases loaded . . . He gets the sign . . . Digs in . . . Runner on second takes a lead . . . Outside, ball one . . . Hamm's, the Beer Refreshing . . . Twenty-mile-an-hour wind coming off the lake . . . Shakes off another . . . Just misses, ball two . . . Gonnella Bread—it's delicious. Have a Gonnella, it's swella, fella! . . . Ernie on deck . . . Billy swings. That's hit! . . . way back . . . back, back, back . . . Hey-hey! All the way onto Waveland Avenue! . . . Everybody up on their feet! They're going crazy, they're going crazy! . . ."

After I grew up, and started making friends with Yankees and Dodgers fans, they'd often ask, "This Cubs . . . thing. I mean, how can you stand to lose, day after day, year after year?" I'd think, no, we always won the World Series on the last play every afternoon, and walked home under the streetlights.

A mong my many blessings in life was that I could feel a couple of personal family links to the Cubs.

Charlie Grimm, the old Cubs manager and former first baseman, was married to one of my mother's best friends, my Auntie Marian. So I got to call the man who managed the Cubs the last time they were in the World Series in 1945 "Uncle Charlie."

He had met Marian when she was the lounge singer at the Club Alabam on Rush Street, and Charlie a devoted customer who could be persuaded to come to the small stage and play his left-handed banjo. He also often played for fans at Wrigley before the game. Charlie Grimm's hands were enormous and looked swollen from the thousands of pegs he'd speared at first base from the likes of Stan Hack and Billy Jurges. They were arresting to see, and Charlie seemed to know it.

"These hands were never meant to hold a briefcase," he'd say, raising them for appraisal. "Just a bat, a glove, a ball, and a banjo." (And, to be sure, an Old Fashioned glass.)

When Uncle Charlie held out the gravy boat at Thanksgiving dinner, it seemed to sink in his hand. When he brought out a pumpkin pie, it looked not much larger than a Kennedy half-dollar in his palm. And yet Charlie Grimm was meticulous. He carved the turkey with the delicacy of a cardiac surgeon. He somehow managed to slip his huge mitt into the turkey carcass and bring out tender slivers. He'd rinse and dry his hands, and I'd see his fingernails glisten. Charlie knew people stared at his hands, so the old showman got regular manicures ("And pretty gals hold your hands," he told me).

He'd bring out one of his banjos after dinner, along with a few stories. "Bing gave me this one," he'd announce over more than one banjo. "He'd come over to Catalina to see us during spring training, before the Dodgers moved west. He gave it to me to settle a poker debt." Auntie Marian—a great jazz singer—would scat-sing along as Charlie played and sang:

I ain't gonna work on the factory
I ain't gonna work on the farm
Lay around the shack 'til the mail train comes back
And I'll roll in my sweet baby's arms

"Charlie—that song—must you—*really?*" I remember my mother asking, with a nod toward me. I was probably about ten or twelve. But she was also laughing.

"Aww, Patsy," Charlie would say, "it's just a song about a guy taking a nap." I believed that until recently, just because that's what Charlie Grimm told me.

And Jack Brickhouse was my godfather. He was the Chicago Cubs announcer for more than thirty years, and my father's best friend and most devoted drinking buddy. Uncle Jack, as I called him, had a huge harvest moon of a face, and just about the best-known voice in Chicago. When we played parking lot baseball, Jack's voice was the one that chimed in our minds, especially his home run call: "That's hit . . . back . . . back . . . Hey-hey!"

(I once told Uncle Jack I'd met a woman in New York who said she deduced that a man grew up in Chicago if he shouted "Hey-hey!" when they reached . . . romantic fruition. Uncle Jack was delighted. For the rest of his life, when we said goodbye he'd lean in to hug me close and whisper, "You keep saying 'Hey-hey,' now, kid . . .")

Jack loved my father. When I was born, two months premature, scrawny and gasping, Uncle Jack ordered another

Early Times for my father and called a rugged-looking guy to meet them at the bar. He said he'd been born premature, too, to an Irish mother who kept warm bricks in his crib; and now George Connor was a Chicago Bears linebacker. They closed down the bar. And after my father had drunk himself out of jobs and his marriage, Uncle Jack still took him to classy spots for lunch, so he could eat well and be funny for a day, and called in favors to try to find him work.

I was sixteen when my father died. Uncle Jack tried to step in, asking my mother if she wanted me to live with his family and attend a famously splendid suburban school along the lakeshore. I wanted to stay with my mother but was touched by Jack's generosity.

I'd sometimes get off the El after seeing the "L" or "W" above Wrigley Field and give my name at the gate. They'd call Uncle Jack, who was often on his second scotch in the Pink Poodle, the ballpark's press lounge, where sportswriters, managers, coaches, and even a few players would find their way after a game. I overheard stories about Babe Ruth ("Sweet until he's drunk. And he was always drunk"), Joe DiMaggio ("I knew it would never last with Marilyn. Joe's never seen a movie that doesn't star Goofy"), and Stan Musial ("Nicest son of a bitch in the world. What's his problem?"). I learned not to like Leo Durocher, the Cubs manager, because he'd never pay for a drink. Uncle Jack never got a bill at the Poodle, but he'd fold a couple of fives under his last round.

"That's what a classy guy does, Scotty," he'd tell me, then point to Leo's empty martini glass, encircled by a litter of olive spears, but no tip. "Not that."

Each fall, Uncle Jack would watch Vin Scully with the Dodgers, Jack Buck and Harry Caray with the Cardinals, and Milo Hamilton of the Braves go off with their teams to announce World Series games. Jack would have to stay at home once the Cubs washed out, with the Pink Poodle closed (he did find other spots). But with few stars and little success to dramatize, Uncle Jack began to enthuse on-air about *beeeautiful* Wrigley Field, the park, the ivy, and the sunshine.

"I'll keep score," he used to tell me. "You just have a good time at the game."

B aseball players on all teams will tell you that they don't believe in curses. But if they get a crucial hit in a game one night, they'll wear the same socks the next.

I have talked to a score of Cubs players over the years and carefully asked about . . . this curse stuff. They answer with a kind of monologue of aplomb: *I was always the best athlete in my town. I pitched a shutout and hit three home runs in our state championship game. I've been a* SportsCenter *highlight. I'm a winner. I'm lucky. That's what got me here. Hard work and skill are real, not curses.*

But a few minutes later, they might talk about what their first thoughts were when they heard they were coming to the Cubs: *Great town. Best park, best fans. You'll never be more popular in your life than you will be on the north side of Chicago. But you hear these stories . . .*

I don't believe in curses. But I do believe (I kind of have to) in the power of stories. And over 108 years, the more the Cubs lost, often in farcical and fantastic ways, the more those losses strengthened the fairy tale that the club must be cursed.

I used to rewrite lines from Carl Sandburg's poem "Chicago" for the Cubs:

Come and show me another city with lifted head singing so proud and loud to be in love with flops so lovable and cunning with excuses

Stinging with magnetic curses amid the toil of piling loss
on loss, here is a tall bold loser struggling just to beat
St. Louis, Cincinnati, and Pittsburgh . . .

Laughing the loony batty bawling whimpering of defeat,
half-faded, sweating, proud to be Hit Butcher, Out
Maker, Stacker of Defeats, Loser by Boatloads and
Curse Sufferer to the Nation!

The Cubs got into and lost six World Series in the thirty-seven years between 1908 and 1945. The Cubs lost the 1910 Series to the Philadelphia Athletics when a great pitcher named Jack Coombs won three of what turned out to be just a five-game series. No curse—just Coombs.

The Cubs lost their next World Series in 1918, to the Boston Red Sox, who won while scoring just nine runs in the six-game series. This is still a record for scoring economy, all the more improbable because Babe Ruth was on that Red Sox team—pitching. He threw 29⅔ consecutive scoreless innings, which stood as a record for forty years. No voodoo, just the Bambino.

Eleven more years would pass before the Cubs had a chance to lose the World Series again, this time to the 1929 Philadelphia Athletics. Hack Wilson, a Cubs Hall of

Fame center fielder (and brawler and carouser, a true triple threat), lost track of fly balls in the sky. When a little boy asked Joe McCarthy, the Cubs manager, for a souvenir baseball, he told him, "Stand behind Wilson. You'd get all the loose balls you want."

The Cubs returned to the World Series in 1932, only to lose in four straight games to the New York Yankees of nine future Hall of Fame players. In the fifth inning of the third game, Babe Ruth stood back from the plate, pointed at the bleachers with a hand, and whacked a Charlie Root curveball five hundred feet, past the center field flag pole. Did the Babe call that home run shot? He certainly encouraged that story over the years. Or had Ruth just made a gesture to bark back at some of the epithets Cubs players hurled at him?

It is hard to question the word of a Supreme Court justice. John Paul Stevens was a twelve-year-old boy at the game that day with his father. He once assured me, "Ruth did point to the center field scoreboard." (I'm pretty sure he didn't mean Justice Ginsburg.) "And he did hit the ball out of the park after he pointed with his bat. So it really happened."

But Charlie Root, who threw the ball, never saw it that way. He'd tell all reporters that if he'd really thought Ruth had boasted about where he would hit his next pitch, "I'd have knocked him on his ass."

Ruth's Called Shot became part of the Babe's legend. But it also entered Chicago Cubs lore as a story to show how the club lost important games in preposterous ways. The most dangerous home run hitter in baseball came to the plate, and what did the Cubs bench do? Razz him until, like King Kong swatting airplanes with the palm of his hand, the Sultan of Swat walloped a home run. Next time, try a little tenderness.

The Cubs returned to the World Series in 1936—and lost in six games to the Detroit Tigers. They had a return engagement with the Yankees in 1938—and lost this series in four straight games, too. The Chicago Cubs had already become a national punch line for loss and frustration by the time William Sianis took his pet goat to Wrigley Field in 1945 for a World Series game.

Bill Sianis came to Chicago as a teenager from Greece in 1912. He washed dishes in the West Loop, and when Prohibition ended in 1933, he reportedly wrote a bad check to buy a storefront near the Chicago stadium that he turned into a bar. He made good on his bad paper within a week.

The Lincoln Tavern was the name of the bar when Bill Sianis bought it. A lot of trucks that hauled livestock would turn down that stretch of West Madison Street on their way to the old Chicago stockyards, and at some point a baby goat fell off of a truck and got brought into the bar.

Billy Goat was a nickname for Bill Sianis, who had a long face, graying hair, and a jagged spike of a beard. He saw the baby goat and apparently got all gooey. What naturalists call "mutual scenting" ensued. Billy Goat nursed the little goat back to health, and the bewhiskered ruminant, which he named Murphy, became his personal mascot. The line between Billy Goat Sianis and the baby goat became almost indistinguishable. Sianis renamed his bar the Billy Goat Tavern.

The 1945 World Series was between the Cubs and the Detroit Tigers. Charlie Grimm was the Cubs manager. Most of baseball's best players still wore uniforms that were more important than baseball jerseys in this last year of World War II, so both clubs were stocked with "rejects and 4Fs who knew it was their last chance at major league ball," said Uncle Charlie. "God, I loved them."

The Cubs were ahead, two games to one, when the teams arrived in Chicago. Billy Goat Sianis bought two box seats for $7.20. Bill Sianis and his goat had become local celebrities and were welcomed into the park. Billy paraded his billy around the infield in a pregame drizzle, Murphy adorned with a placard that said WE GOT DETROIT'S GOAT.

Ushers tried to convince Bill Sianis that he'd had his fun, and gotten shots of Murphy into the next day's newspapers, but now it was time for man and goat to go. Billy Goat produced the two box seat tickets. By the fourth inning, a couple of cops had joined the ushers to tell Billy that fans had complained about the smell of Murphy's sopping fur. I'm not sure Cubs fans should talk.

William Sianis was offended. The Cubs had welcomed Billy and his billy goat as free pregame entertainment. But the Cubs didn't consider them fit company to stay for the game? All the beers he had poured for the ushers and cops who had come to the Billy Goat Tavern, where Billy would never give them a bill. "Hey, no, on the house." All the times Billy had brought Murphy to kids' birthday parties and Police Athletic League picnics. Then they get hauled out of Wrigley Field like shoplifters?

Wouldn't that make you almost want to lay down a curse on the club you loved?

Some people on the scene insist that as Billy and Murphy were hustled out of the park, Bill Sianis huffed something like, "There will never be another World Series at Wrigley Field." Charlie Grimm said that he and the players heard nothing. Some members of the Sianis family have claimed Bill sent a telegram to Phil Wrigley: "You are going to lose this World Series and never play in any other World Series because you insulted my goat."

Whatever Billy Goat Sianis said or didn't, the Cubs lost the World Series to Detroit, four games to three. Billy Goat told reporters in subsequent years that he sent Phil Wrigley another telegram: "Who stinks now?" The Cubs would not play in a World Series again for seventy-one years. And any time the team seemed on a course to the World Series, or even a few outs away, incredible and unforeseen events—black cats, or the hand of a fan—seemed to strike like bolts of lightning from a blue sky.

Curses are ridiculous fictions that prey upon the faithful and the feebleminded. Which made us Cub fans vulnerable.

My father took me to the Billy Goat when I was growing up and spent weekends with him in his room at the St. Clair Hotel, just east of Michigan Avenue.

The St. Clair was one of the old show business hotels near the Rush Street nightclub district, where itinerant comics, including my father, chorus dancers, jazzmen, working girls, and retired mob gunsels lived in single rooms furnished with a sofa bed (where I slept, while my father dozed in an armchair), a single-burner hot plate, and a knee-high refrigerator that could just about hold a carton of orange juice, from which my father and I would swig directly, so as not to have to rinse cups in the bathroom sink.

By that time, Bill Sianis had moved the Billy Goat to its current location, a small, snug space just below Michigan Avenue, just a few thoughtful steps from all four of the city's major daily newspapers. My father would point out reporters to me, drinking, smoking, laughing, coughing, boasting, and wheezing over their beers, as if we were watching deer feed at a salt lick. Billy Goat Sianis often held court in a corner while his nephew, Sam, worked the bar, and other Sianises and friends of the Sianises from their villages in Greece would peel thin hamburger patties from stacks of waxed paper and slap them into the hot sputter of the old steel griddle.

Sam Sianis would spritz my Pepsi into a beer mug and add a wedge of lime on a tiny green plastic spear and a red plastic straw. "Here you go, young man, full service." He

would discreetly top off my father's Pepsi with a shot of vodka, so when I came back to my mother's apartment on Sunday night, I could tell her, "Dad? Oh, he just had a few Pepsis." I suppose I had figured out by the age of twelve or thirteen that my father was drinking himself to death. He would desperately slurp the last, slick drops on the ice in his glass—a man doesn't do that just for a Pepsi—and signal for another while the glass was still in his lips.

I also suppose I could have told my mother that my father was drinking in front of me. But I was sure this would force her to tell him he couldn't see me until he stopped, and I knew he would promise that he had, even as we all knew he hadn't, and I didn't want to tell on my father and set off more of his lies and my mother's hurt and tears because they really did love me and each other. I like to think that if I truly thought that telling on him could stop my father from drinking and save his life, I would have done it. But by then I also knew that though my father loved us fiercely, he mostly lived to drink. That's a real curse.

The Chicago Cubs went into a tailspin after their defeat in the 1945 World Series. They finished third in 1946, sixth in 1947, and dead-solid last in 1948. Norman

Rockwell, the noted artist, went to a doubleheader against the Cubs at Boston Braves Field on May 23, 1948. He sketched assiduously as the Cubs lost both games, 8–5, then 12–4.

The result was Rockwell's September 4, 1948, *Saturday Evening Post* cover, *The Dugout*. Front and center is the beleaguered-looking Cubs manager, Charlie Grimm, slumping, scowling, and holding a hand to his jaw in despair. Bob Rush, the pitcher, is on Charlie's left; Al Walker, the catcher, is to his right. The forlorn batboy (Frank McNulty, a Boston batboy who had to be cajoled into wearing a Cubs uniform for Rockwell) is especially heart-twisting. The boy looks stricken, as if his favorite player has just slipped on a bat, split his pants, and struck out.

The power is all in the unseen insinuation. Who knows what has made them all wince? The Cubs were capable of any clumsiness. Even the towels and glove hanging on the dugout wall look bedraggled.

Charlie Grimm *hated* that painting. "I look like a basset hound," he complained. Looking back on it, I think Charlie, who was a gifted natural comedian, mostly *pretended* to hate Rockwell's painting. He knew it had placed his face into coffee table art books and museum gift shop prints.

Most Cubs fans didn't much like Rockwell's painting when they saw it on the cover of *The Saturday Evening Post*. But over the years, like Uncle Charlie, they felt pride to see the Cubs enshrined in a work of art, however humiliating.

Marian said Rockwell once told them that it wasn't the Cubs, and certainly not Charlie, whom he mocked in the painting. It was the spitting, sputtering fans in the front rows above the dugout. I remember Charlie pointing to a face in the left-hand corner of a print in an art book.

"Recognize that SOB?" I did not. "The awww-tist. Himself," said Charlie, who'd then flip to the book's back flap and the photo of the pipe-smoking painter. It did look a bit like the man he'd painted, jeering in the second row.

"That's the tipoff," said Charlie. "Rockwell went back to this small New England town where he lived and painted in all of his neighbors as fans. He couldn't make fun of them if he didn't put himself in there, too."

But Rockwell's work became a sore spot with fans as the Cubs grew into their watercolored image as emblematic losers. An art dealer once called me for help in getting word to Cubs owner Tom Ricketts that a couple of studies Rockwell drew for the painting were for sale. He thought

Mr. Ricketts might like them for his own. "I didn't want anything to do with it then," Tom told me after the 2016 World Series. "Now I can just say it's part of our history."

Although I have to believe in the power of art, there was a more compelling reason why the Cubs continued to lose through the years Rockwell endearingly depicted. Jackie Robinson became the first African-American player in the major leagues in April 1947. Larry Doby followed with the Cleveland Indians three months later, then Hank Thompson of the St. Louis Browns. But the Cubs didn't sign Ernie Banks and Gene Baker, their first black players, until 1953 (the Yankees, if you're keeping score, didn't integrate until 1955).

Baseball should never have been segregated. But when the walls began to come down, the Cubs should have been among the first teams, not the ninth, to recruit stars from the old Negro League. They could have signed some of finest ballplayers of the time and won plenty. It was only the curse of their own bigotry that held back the Cubs of the forties and fifties.

By the way: there was a tie made of Rockwell's painting. Uncle Jack Brickhouse wore his in his coffin, and I wore mine to be one of his pallbearers. I remember my mother making a flummoxed face and asking, "Darling, did you have to dress like the corpse?"

Ernie Banks became the Cubs' one genuine star through much of this time. He turned out to be one of the most luminous stars in baseball history. Banks was one of the last players from Satchel Paige's old Kansas City Monarchs to be signed for the majors. At shortstop, Ernie had what Uncle Jack called soft hands: balls seemed to waft into his palms and stick to his fingers. He was muscular but skinny. A bat could look too heavy in his arms. But Ernie's slender wrists gave his bat the snap of a buggy whip and some of the compact ferocity of a Jack Dempsey punch. Ernie Banks won home run titles and the Most Valuable Player award in 1958 and 1959, then another home run title in 1960.

But as Ernie's contemporaries Mickey Mantle, Willie Mays, Henry Aaron, and Sandy Koufax played on the main stage of the World Series, Ernie Banks had to create his own light with the Cubs. He became known by his greeting "What a *beeeautiful* day for a ball game! Let's play two today!" (which Ernie once told me he didn't recall saying until it became his personal slogan; it might have been something he muttered after a brushback pitch). As the performance of the Cubs plunged, the love of fans revolved around the sunniness of Ernie Banks. They began to call him Mr. Cub.

I got to interview Ernie Banks a few times over the years and found him genuinely sincere. But he could have more sting than you'd figure for his image. We were getting set up for a recording once when a bystander told him, "All those years losing with the Cubs, and you still go into the Hall of Fame on the first ballot."

"They must have given me extra points for suffering," said Mr. Cub.

The story of Ken Hubbs is where all complaints of curses have to be silent in memory of a real tragedy. Kenny Hubbs was a young legend on the playing fields of Southern California, where he could pitch with either hand and dunk a basketball behind his head.

The priests at Notre Dame tried to recruit Ken Hubbs to play quarterback, Ken's devout Mormonism be damned, or, anyhow, overlooked. Coach John Wooden tried to get him to play guard for UCLA. Ken chose to try profes-

sional baseball instead, and attended Brigham Young in the off-season.

The Cubs signed Ken Hubbs with a $50,000 bonus in 1959, an enormous amount at the time. He breezed through the minor league teams of a last-place club and opened the season with the Cubs in 1962, when he was twenty. In his rookie year, Ken Hubbs hit .260, and handled 418 straight fielding plays over 78 straight games without an error, a major league record. When he was named Rookie of the Year, Phil Wrigley called Ken Hubbs to his office to tear up his contract and double his salary. That was the powerful effect Ken Hubbs seemed to have on people. He made even Phil Wrigley smile to spend more money.

Wrigley recognized that Ken Hubbs was a singular spirit. He lingered on the field to sign autographs and chat with fans. He made unheralded visits to the children's wards of hospitals. His promise continued through the 1963 season. The Cubs still lost twice as many games as they won, but they faced a future with Ernie Banks at short, Ron Santo at third, Billy Williams in right field, and Lou Brock in center field (who would all go into the Hall of Fame)—and Kenny Hubbs, a golden-boy Californian at second base.

Of course nothing is guaranteed. Life was about to demonstrate that in the most awful way.

Ken Hubbs had used part of his new salary to buy a Cessna. On February 15, 1964, Ken Hubbs and a fellow BYU student, Dennis Doyle, crashed in the sleet of a winter storm. He was twenty-two.

Ken Hubbs had an All-Star team of pallbearers, including Ron Santo, Billy Williams, and Ernie Banks. Mayor Richard J. Daley said, "There isn't a man in Chicago who wouldn't have been proud to have him as a son." Charlie Grimm was brokenhearted when he got back from the funeral, and said, to try to make himself laugh, "Ballplayers should be in bars, not flying airplanes."

It sounds squalid just to talk about how his loss may have put the play of the Cubs into a tailspin. But Ken Hubbs was a competitive athlete and would understand. The Cubs had closed out the 1963 season believing that at last they had the heart of a winning ball club. The death of Ken Hubbs tore a hole in that heart.

On June 15 during the 1964 season, the Cubs made a trade so bad that the two names involved are still a duo, enshrined as a phrase to describe blunder: *Brock for*

Broglio. Lou Brock, the Cubs' swift and stylish center fielder, was traded for a St. Louis Cardinals pitcher, Ernie Broglio.

Broglio was twenty-eight, had won eighteen games the year before, and threw what Billy Williams called a "12 to 6" curve that could drop like a depth charge. Lou Brock was twenty-four and fretted that the Cubs might send him back to the minors.

The Cubs couldn't replace Ken Hubbs in the firmament. But they might make a trade to put star power back into their lineup.

Brock for Broglio. Lou Brock got to the Cardinals and batted .348. They would win two World Series and three pennants with Lou Brock in left, who would steal a record 938 bases during his career. Cubs fans can't forget that the man who became Mr. Cardinal is a Cub they traded away.

Ernie Broglio won four games and lost seven for the Cubs in 1964, and was out of baseball by 1966. *Brock for Broglio.*

Cubs fans are tempted to revise the famous verse Franklin P. Adams wrote in 1910 in despair of the Cubs' double-play trio of Tinker to Evers to Chance:

These are the saddest of possible words:
Brock for Broglio in a trade.

A swap 'tween Cubs and Cards that's one for the Birds,
Brock for Broglio in a trade.
Ruthlessly pricking our Cubby Blue bubble,
As Brock turns so many singles into doubles—
Words that are heavy with nothing but trouble:
Brock for Broglio is the trade.

The death of Ken Hubbs was a tragedy. The Brock-for-Broglio trade was a mistake. But each event seemed to encourage the idea that the Cubs were in the orbit of some dark star. They sign the greatest of young players, only to lose him in the most sorrowful way. They trade for a star who flames out as soon as he dons Cubby blue, and then see the underachieving player they sent away catch fire. There is no such thing as a curse. But how else could Cubs fans explain so many decades of failure and frustration?

But it was also during these years that the Cubs began to become a national baseball brand. The Yankees and Dodgers won. The Cubs usually—often comically—lost. But the Cubs became the anti-Yanks. While the Yankees and the Dodgers were corporate flagships among baseball teams, the Cubs were part of a candy store (or at least the Wrigley chewing gum company).

You began with the park: *beeeauuutiful Wrigley Field*, as Uncle Jack pronounced it at the beginning of each game. Wrigley and Boston's Fenway Park were among the last of the neighborhood ballyards. Wrigley was built of red brick, like the walls of an old fire or police station, or a thousand apartment blocks on the north side. Inside, the brick in the outfield was garbed in bright green ivy. The park's pocket-sized dimensions and close seats could make Wrigley Field feel as friendly as a children's sandbox. Home runs (alas, usually from other teams) could smash through apartment windows across the street, just like a home run hit by a ten-year-old playing ball in a parking lot. *Excuse me, Mr. Aaron, but who's going to pay for that window?*

As a lot of modern baseball began to rile fans with co-lossal salaries, cold, soulless stadiums, and owners who up-rooted franchises for tax breaks, the Cubs were a team with a sense of place. That club, in their park, across from the fire station, on the north side of Chicago, seemed to many exactly what a national pastime ought to be.

The Cubs promoted a day at the park as family enter-tainment. But over the years, with their daytime games beamed across the country and even around the world on cable and satellite, I also began to see Cubs games as a pastime that linked solitary souls on lonely afternoons.

I think of my father (and sometimes it's almost too painful to think of him) awake and exhausted at two in the afternoon, in our small, faded hotel room, the Cubs playing on as one more drink dwindled down at his elbow. Many times, in many places, I've wandered into a dark bar on a sunny day, to ask for directions or use the bathroom, and seen a scattering of strangers, roosting two or three seats apart from one another, watching the game from Wrigley Field on the screen overhead, the voice of Jack Brickhouse, Harry Caray, or Len Kasper keeping them company: *Dawson coming up . . . Flied to right last time, on with a walk in the second . . . Tuesday is Cubs Refrigerator Magnet Day at the park . . . That's low and outside, ball one . . . Cubs down by two . . .*

For Cubs fans, the 1969 season is bittersweet, the story of a love too painful to recall, but too briefly blissful to forget. Leo Durocher, a legend who had managed miracles with the New York Giants but often couldn't manage himself, had come in from the restless boredom of enforced retirement in Beverly Hills, married a local Chicago girl, Lynn Walker Goldblatt Durocher, and helped manage the Cubs to a sensational start.

The Cubs won eleven of their first twelve games. They had what looked to be the strongest team in the field, with an aging Ernie Banks now moved to first, Ron Santo at third, Randy Hundley behind the plate, Don Kessinger at short, Billy Williams and Jim Hickman in the outfield, and splendid starting pitchers in Fergie Jenkins, Ken Holtzman, and Bill Hands.

It was the first summer after my father died, when I felt that I had, in the words of Corinthians, put away childish things. In the summer of 1969, I wanted a few of them back. When the Cubs won on so many afternoons, Ron Santo would run off the field and click his heels, like a Russian folk dancer. "Hey-hey!" Uncle Jack would shout. "Santo's dance!" Some of the Cubs went into a north side studio and recorded a song for charity:

Hey-hey, holy mackerel, no doubt about it!
The Cubs are on their way!

We translated our new civic anthem in my Spanish class:

Hey-hey, sagrado mackerel, sin ninguna duda!
Los Cachorros estan el camino!

On Sunday, July 20, while the Cubs were winning both ends of a doubleheader against the Philadelphia Phillies, man landed on the moon. A group of us grade school friends watched Buzz and Neil bounce on the moon's surface like circus bears. It was the middle of the night by the time my friend Avi and I walked out on the street to catch the 151 bus, and the world was at home, amazed and dreaming of what we had all seen. Avi and I waved up at the moon. Maybe someone would now wave back.

"Our kids will live there one day," Avi told me. "The world will get a fresh start."

There was a newspaper vending machine at the bus stop and I bought the *Sun-Times*. There was MAN ON THE MOON on the front, CUBS IN FIRST PLACE on the back. That seemed about right.

Ken Holtzman, often called Chicago's Sandy Koufax, threw a no-hitter against the Atlanta Braves on August 19. It put the Cubs 8½ games ahead of the Cardinals and 9½ games over the New York Mets. Cubs fans began to think we had to worry about whether Kenny Holtzman would refuse to pitch on Yom Kippur, too.

But then came the September swoon that would make the Cubs perhaps the most famous second-place team in baseball history. The Cubs got tired. Leo Durocher believed in putting his best nine players on the field, day after day, even in the August sun, all talk of rest and substitution being pantywaist mumbo-jumbo.

"Leo did it with the Giants and Dodgers, if you take a look," Uncle Jack told me one afternoon at the Pink Poodle. "Win lots of games early, when no one else is going all out, and put yourself ahead. But then, when you need the steam in September, the boiler is bare."

The Mets, with an amazin' pitching staff that included Tom Seaver, Jerry Koosman, and a young Nolan Ryan (scary thought, that), caught the wind while the Cubs hobbled. The two teams were facing each other on September 9, Seaver on the mound in the second inning, when a black cat walked past Ron Santo in the on-deck circle. It arched its back. Then the cat sauntered to the Cubs dugout to hiss at Leo Durocher. "Can't blame a cat for that," Leo said later. The Mets won, 7–1, and the Cubs never saw first place again. The New York Mets won their first World Series that year.

Leo Durocher took up smoking again that night, and as he took a long drag in the dugout the Cubs equipment manager, Yosh Kawano, told him, "Those things will kill you."

"That's the general idea," said Leo.

The Cubs were already in a nosedive in the summer of 1969 and didn't need a black cat to cross their path. They didn't need Da Curse when they had Durocher. But no one ever claimed the small black cat at security after the game, and he had to be turned over to a city shelter. I like to think they gave the cat a World Series ring, not a needle.

Theories wise and wild on why the Cubs lost abounded during this period. They spent money. They stocked their roster. They had sellout crowds. So what baleful force (*the quality of Cubness*) kept the Cubs from winning?

Was the answer in lights?

For most of the time after it was built in 1914, Wrigley Field had no lights. When I told this to my wife, she asked, "So no one could see what was going on?"

Actually, it was principle, or the gospel according to Phil Wrigley, who said, "We believe that baseball is a daytime sport and will continue to play it in the sunshine as long as we can. Let there *not* be lights." *In the beginning, there was green ivy on the redbrick walls of the playing field. And the lake winds blew across the outfield. And Phil Wrigley said, "Let there* not *be lights."*

Every few years, a new Cubs general manager would remark that the Cubs could not compete for players unless they could increase their team's revenues with commercials in prime-time (nighttime) television. Mr. Wrigley would just as quickly knock down such speculation. But a couple of other forces weren't so easy to rebuff.

The ballpark's neighborhood began to change. A neighborhood of families who worked long hours in factories and warehouses began to become prime territory for youngish urban professionals who worked long hours in the banks, showcase shops, ad agencies, hospitals, and law firms of the Loop and North Michigan Avenue. Realtors coined the word *Wrigleyville*. The settlers liked the brio and dash of living near Wrigley, and cared less about quiet streets by 10:00 p.m.

Then the *Chicago Tribune* bought the team in 1981. The *Trib* was Republican by history and conviction and had a principle, as strong as Mr. Wrigley's: a company doesn't buy a major sports franchise to lose money.

Trib executives warned that if the Cubs ever did reach the World Series, the team might have to honor the national prime-time television contract by playing their home games in *St. Louis*. Or maybe the *Trib* would have to build a new ballpark in a suburb that would welcome the Cubs with bright lights and tax breaks. Would they call it Richard Nixon Field?

As decades of day-only baseball went on, a lot of Cubs fans (myself included) may have become a little too proud of Wrigley Field's antique appeal. We confused charm with character. We acted like we wanted to keep Wrigley preserved inside some baseball diorama, in which games are played in sunlight, bleacher seats are just a buck, and Babe Ruth might duck-walk to the plate to call his shot into center field. We seemed to care more about keeping lights out of Wrigley Field than putting a good team onto the field. As Mark Grace, the Cubs first baseman, said, "Sometimes I think this isn't a baseball team, it's a theme park."

(I had another idea during this period: that the Cubs play night games at Wrigley *without* lights. Audio engineers could play sounds of the crack of a bat and roars from a crowd, while an actual Cubbies crowd drank beer and had a wonderful time in oblivious darkness. I'm not sure Harry Caray would have noticed.)

Another question began to bedevil Cubs fans: What if day games were to blame for their defeats?

The Cubs played day baseball at home, but in the cool of the night out-of-town. Concerned physicians came forward to say the constant adjustments the Cubs had to make between day and night games could throw off their delicately balanced biometrics. It could make them . . . *irregular*. A Prunes for the Bruins campaign invited fans to send a laxative to a favorite Cubs player. *Fortune favors the regular.* Wrigley's mailroom got flush, if you please, with packets of Ex-Lax, Swiss Kriss, and pitted prunes. If Ryne Sandberg looked a little slow to get down for a grounder, I'd tell myself, "He must feel a little bloated."

Another worry about day baseball was the way it fit too beautifully into Chicago's prodigious nightlife. A player could be showered, scented, and free to raise hell by 5:00 p.m., which is a tough training regimen if you want to win a pennant. Chicago's plentitude of clubs made it a favorite stop for visiting teams, but the cycle of playing and partying may have defeated the hometown club.

Sunshine baseball is also one thing in April, when flowers bloom and cheeks are rosy. It can be quite another in August, when everything and everybody, including the ivy on Wrigley's walls, begins to wilt.

I was supposed to meet friends at the first night game played in Wrigley Field in August 1988. But we couldn't find each other before the game, and I wound up watching in a Wrigleyville bar. It was stupefying to see Wrigley Field aglow for the first time. It was almost a surprise to see that the ballpark still stood at night at Clark and Addison.

Rick Sutcliffe, the Cub who threw the first pitch of that game, told me later that the vast pop of light from thousands of flashbulbs trying to capture the first nighttime pitch nearly knocked him off the mound. A man on a perch nearby announced to everyone at the bar, "Well, there goes the neighborhood!" The bartender said, "I hope so."

The Cubs were ahead 3–1 in the fourth inning when the heavens opened and rained down their outrage over night baseball at Wrigley Field. The game was called. It has therefore never appeared in the record books. How could Cubs fans see their lead washed away forever by fierce rains and not believe some curse was at work?

Today the Cubs can play thirty-five night games a season in Wrigley Field, a fine balance between tradition, necessity, and the neighborhood. Any proposal to reduce that number would probably provoke an uprising of tavern owners. Two-thirds of all home games are still played in daylight, but in August Joe Maddon often cancels batting practice, which he calls "the most overrated component in major league baseball." That must cover a lot of possibilities.

I don't believe clinging to daytime baseball was to blame for a century of Cubs losses. But over decades, day games hardened into a purposeless principle. The Cubs didn't need to bring night games to Wrigley Field to finally win a World Series. But those of us who are fans probably needed to decide whether we wanted a real baseball team on the north side of town, or to remain day-trippers to a kind of baseball Never-Never Land.

The Cubs began another fifth-place season in the spring of 1983 with an especially abysmal start: five wins and fourteen losses. They lost to the Los Angeles Dodgers one April afternoon, 4–3, and their manager, Lee Elia, heard boos from the stands. He was on full boil by the time he reached the locker room.

Elia delivered a rant that actors today could use for an audition monologue. It is breathtakingly profane, with patches of eloquence. Its explosive quality is actually more graphic with asterisks.

After hearing boos and curses, Lee Elia told reporters,

SCOTT SIMON

"F**k those f**kin' fans who come out here and say they're Cub fans that are supposed to be behind you rippin' every f**kin' thing you do. I'll tell you one f**kin' thing, I hope we get f**kin' hotter than s**t, just to stuff it up them three thousand f**kin' people that show up every f**kin' day, because if they're the real Chicago f**kin' fans, they can kiss my f**kin' ass right downtown and *print it.*"

Oh, they did. A radio reporter had his recorder running, too. Having limbered up his tongue, Lee Elia went on to call the fans who paid to watch his flailing ball club the true losers:

". . . The motherf**kers don't even work. That's why they're out at the f**kin' game. They oughta go out and get a f**kin' job and find out what it's like to go out and earn a f**kin' living. Eighty-five percent of the f**kin' world is working. The other fifteen percent come out here. A f**kin' playground for the c******kers. Rip them motherf**kers. Rip them f**kin' c******kers like the f**kin' players. We got guys bustin' their f**kin' ass, and them f**kin' people boo. And that's the Cubs?"

Elia ended his fulminations by doing what good managers are supposed to: deflecting pressure from his players.

"What I'm tryin' to say is don't rip them f**kn' guys out there. Rip me. If you wanna rip somebody, rip my

58

f**kin' ass. But don't rip them f**kin' guys 'cause they're givin' everything they can give."

Elia uttered a profanity (usually the same old one, just in different configurations) every three seconds. The radio reporter played the rant for Cubs management for their comment. Dallas Green, the Cubs' GM, called Elia to his office. They listened together, Green seething. He had brought Elia to Chicago for his competitive fire. Now his manager had turned a torch on the fans who had supported a failing club for so long.

"I surprised myself," Elia says now. "I didn't realize half of what I had said. I was like, 'Where in the world did I come up with that?'"

Lee apologized to Dallas Green on the spot. He also said he had to leave to umpire his daughter's softball game in Park Ridge (with presumably less picturesque language). Green gave his old friend the benefit of delaying what they both knew must be his dismissal. The Cubs arranged for Lee Elia to be interviewed by Jack Brickhouse on the radio that night, and Elia was contrite. Uncle Jack told me later, "The condemned man and I went out for drinks later and I asked him, 'What the f**k were you thinking?'"

It was very Cubs-like: curses, comedy, losses, and embarrassment.

All these years later, there's something appealing about Lee Elia's rant. He was fiercely loyal to his players. Lee went on to manage a few minor league teams, doing just well enough to go on to another job on a lower rung. He is good-humored and approachable about the event for which he's best remembered, and will even record curses for charities.

(I have met members of Dallas Green's family. His nine-year-old granddaughter, Christina, was a bright and sweet youngster, interested in politics, who went to a Tucson shopping center to meet her representative in Congress, Gabrielle Giffords, in January 2011. Christina-Taylor Green died when a deranged gunman opened fire and killed six people.)

For decades, the only other team that could compare to the Cubs for futility was the Boston Red Sox, who had won their last World Series in 1918. But when Bill Buckner, the Cubs' able first baseman, was traded to the Red Sox, he arrived just in time to be on the 1986 team that faced the New York Mets in the World Series. The Red Sox were an out from winning the World Series when

Mookie Wilson of the Mets hit what the announcer Vin Scully called a "little roller up along first."

Buckner got his glove down on the ground to make the out. But the little roller skipped through his legs. A run scored, and the Red Sox lost all.

Buckner, who has rerun that play in his mind at least as much as any inconsolable Red Sox fan, figured out over the years that his old glove just flopped closed too soon.

But when analysts went over the video and photos of Bill Buckner's gaffe, they saw something else: Buckner wore an old blue Cubs batting glove under his mitt. *If the glove fits, the curse transmits.*

The Chicago Cubs were just five outs from going to the World Series in 2003 when Luis Castillo of the Florida Marlins sliced a short fly ball down the left field line. It looked like a routine foul, and the Cubs seemed to be on cruise control. They were ahead, 3–0, three games to two, in the eighth inning of game six of the National League Championship Series. Mark Prior, Kerry Wood's slightly junior partner in the dreamy mound duo sportswriters called Chicago Heat, was working on a two-hit game.

SCOTT SIMON

The foul ball began to fall from the sky over the sloping brick wall that runs alongside the third base line. Moisés Alou, the Cubs' left fielder, leapt up and opened his glove to catch the ball just as it arrived in aisle 4, row 8, over seat 13. A twenty-six-year-old man in glasses, a Cubs cap, and a black Renegades sweatshirt (for the youth baseball team he coached) also tried to catch that ball. That man's name is now as famous as if he had been in a Kipling poem:

> You may talk o' hot dogs and beer
> When the score of the game is drear
> An' you're wonderin' why the Cubs canna' win the
>   Series . . .
> But of all the Cubby fans we knew
> The name that brings most ballyhoo
> Is the guy who became a goat, Steven Bartman,
> It's still Bartman! Bartman! Bartman!
> That goofus in the headphones, Steven Bartman!

The foul ball bounced around the seats. Moisés Alou slammed his mitt against his thigh. Mark Prior pointed out the man under the headphones to the umpires, to complain of fan interference. The video of that *episode* (it really wasn't a play) has been replayed, frame by frame—and this is a tasteless analogy, I know, but true—almost as much as the Zapruder film.

My wife and I were watching in a bar. I tried to look unshaken.

"These things happen," I announced (while screaming inside like a lost little boy). "We're ahead. We'll be fine."

Or whatever Rommel said just before the invasion of Normandy.

On the screen behind the bottles of single malt scotch and Cherry Noir vodka, Mark Prior threw a wild pitch, which sent Castillo to first base. Iván Rodríguez singled home Juan Pierre. Twenty-year-old Miguel Cabrera hit a grounder to short that had *double-play ball* written in red stitching across the seams. But Alex Gonzalez, a fine fielder, bobbled the ball as if it were an unraveling ball of yarn. The bases were loaded. Then Derrek Lee came up and slapped a double, Florida tied the score, and the chill began to move up my spine.

The Florida Marlins would go on to score 8 runs in the inning and win the game, 8–3. My wife and I watched the seventh game, and Kerry Wood started strong, even hitting a home run. I leapt up and shouted in the Friendly Confines of our apartment, "Kerry Wood comes to play! Kerry is the man!"

Yet I think most Cubs fans watched that seventh game with spirit, but no faith. We didn't wait for a grand slam, but the next debacle. We may not have believed in curses, but had learned to expect fiascos. As Allen Ginsberg might have put it—

I saw the best minds of my generation destroyed by the
madness of being a Cubs fan,
Starving for victory, hysterical, naked in cold lake winds,
Dragging ourselves through north side streets at dawn
looking
For the fix of one lousy run,
Angelheaded losers burning for the ancient ivied
Connection to the starry dynamo phenom that only the
Yankees ever seem to sign.

My wife heard muffled gasps in the bathroom early the next morning. She crept to the door, turned the handle, and found me sobbing into a towel. She asked, but knew, "What's wrong?" I looked at the woman I love and felt twelve again. I told her, "But I thought we really had a chance this year!" and let the towel drop from my chin because I had to sob.

A number of the people who sat near Bartman that night told Alex Gibney, who directed the fine film *Catching Hell* for ESPN, that they had moved to try to catch Castillo's ball, too. A couple of inches to the right or left, and they might have been Bartmans. They think Moisés Alou was too far below the wall to catch that foul ball. Alou himself, a six-time All-Star, has always said the ball was on its way into his glove. "I'm convinced one hundred percent," he told Gibney.

But Moisés has never blamed Steve Bartman for the Cubs' defeat. "The Marlins," he's said, "bang, bang, bang, suddenly, that inning, it was like batting practice."

Most Cubs fans have seen the video of this sequence over the years more than *Law & Order* reruns. Here is what I've come to believe:

Steve Bartman did not commit fan interference. Umpires were right not to make that call. His hands never broke the invisible line over the field of play. But I also think Bartman's reach for the ball prevented Moisés Alou from being able to catch it. That's where *mights* and *what-ifs* take over.

What if Alou had been able to catch that foul for the

second out of the inning? Mark Prior would not have had to throw another pitch to Luis Castillo. There would not have been a wild pitch for a walk to let the Marlins take first base. If Miguel Cabrera had still hit a ground ball to short, Alex Gonzales would not have had to rush to turn the ball into a double play. He might have gotten Cabrera at first to end the inning there. The Marlins might have scored just one run, not eight. The Chicago Cubs might well have been in the World Series. *What if, what if, might, might, might.*

I'm more intrigued by another question: What if Moisés Alou hadn't slammed his mitt, skulked in a circle, and then stalked back to left field?

Alou was entitled to be angry. But his show of fury made it look as if Steve Bartman had grabbed defeat from the jaws of victory over his glove. What if Moisés had just shrugged off a fan's stab for a foul ball with a wry, resigned smile? When you see the video, you begin to catch how Alou's reaction riled the crowd in Wrigley Field. And it's that reaction, then the sullen faces and smoldering quiet, that may have made young Cubs who thought they didn't believe in the curse start to wonder, "Is this the scourge I've heard so much about? A billy goat, a black cat, and now a guy who looks like he's hearing signals from space aliens?"

You don't have to believe in curses for a curse to find you.

There was also a worse ugliness that night. People in the stands began to chant a singsong of "Ass-hole! Ass-hole!" A few people threw cups of beer. Bartman wiped suds from his eyes with the back of his hand, and tried with great dignity to watch the game. Some of the shouts became truly vile. A small chorus shouted, "We're gonna kill you!"

After a few minutes, Wrigley security guards and Chicago police were able to make it to aisle 4, row 8, seat 13, and help Steve Bartman and two friends safely escape from the park of the team he loved. There were shouts, shoves, and flattened popcorn boxes hurled his way. Bartman finally hung his coat over his head while eight or more guards tried to steer him through ranks of sputtering, spitting halfwits in Cubs hats. It was disgraceful and sickening, and should be especially so to Cubs fans. That night, *we* did not deserve to get into the World Series.

Police in the suburb where Steve Bartman lived with his parents had to throw up a police line to protect him. But, contrary to folklore, there is no evidence he ever moved away.

Of course Governor Rod Blagojevich had one of the most shameless reactions. He said of Steve Bartman, "The guy would never get a pardon from me." But former governor Blagojevich is now in prison for trying to auction off the U.S. Senate seat once held by Barack Obama. He has more sympathy for pardons.

Steve Bartman reportedly works in a financial services firm, and declines all requests for interviews through Frank Murtha, a sports agent and family friend who represents him without pay. Steve has loyal and supportive friends who want you to know: he's nice, he's not mad, he's doing fine, and he's still a Cubs fan.

Steve Bartman has been offered a lot of money over the years for commercials and appearances. He has refused them all. The Cubs have honored his request to simply be left alone. As Frank Murtha says, "He has one desire in all this: at some point, to see it end."

In a time when people don't blush to get rich by cashing in on the notoriety of sex videos, there is something noble about Steve Bartman's meticulous anonymity. As a Kipling poem might put it:

> So we'll meet 'im later on
> At Wrigley in some misty dawn—
> Where we can point to all the spots a ball was dropped.
> E'll be squatting in seat one-thirteen

An' finally catch a foul ball clean
An' at last we'll clean the slate for Steven Bartman!
So it's Bartman! Bartman! Bartman!
The name we cry in nightmares, Steven Bartman!
Though we've cussed you and we've cursed you,
By the livin' Gawd that made you,
You're a better fan than I am, Steven Bartman!

I do not believe in curses. But I like the idea of karma, or at least the notion that good acts can lead to good results and bad acts won't. The Chicago Cubs didn't deserve to be in the World Series in 2003 if they couldn't come back from a debacle that lead to a breakdown and win game seven. They didn't deserve to be in the World Series that year because Sammy Sosa was in right field. He charmed and enthralled Cubs fans and the country with his home run records, and all the while he deceived us by using banned drugs and then lied about it like a politician, under oath before the U.S. Congress. (The less said about Sammy Sosa, the better.)

And they didn't deserve to get into the World Series in 2003 because too many Cubs fans ridiculed and threatened a good man, Steve Bartman, just for behaving like a fan. In 2003, Cubs fans put a curse on our own team.

• • •

I've been honored to throw out the first pitch at Wrigley Field a couple of times, the distinction diluted only a little in knowing that with eighty-one home games a year, most people and probably several house pets will eventually be invited to throw out the first pitch, too.

The first time, I embarrassed my wife, my daughters, and probably even my late mother. The day before the game, my old grade school battery mate, Lewie Karp, joined me in Lincoln Park. We warmed up with a game of catch. Our shoulders made sounds like a troupe of Spanish dancers.

Then we stepped off an imprecise sixty feet and six inches, the distance from pitcher's mound to home plate. I thought of the scene in *Hoosiers* where coach Gene Hackman has his shortest player sit on the shoulder of his stoutest to run a tape measure from the floor up to the basketball hoop, to tell his team of small-town boys about to play for the state championship in a vast Indianapolis field house, "Ten feet—just like our gym back in Hickory."

Sixty feet, six inches, just like Wrigley Field. Hey, Lew, let's throw this pitch for all the dorky guys just like us!

Lewie got into a half crouch, and I threw. I scudded a

few into his feet, and a couple over Lew's head, but mostly got the ball there—albeit as soft as a marshmallow sundae—and into the silhouette of a strike zone. *Way to chuck it, Scooter! Way to grab it, Lewie!* Lew slipped his hand from his mitt and pretended it was red and throbbing. We felt like mini-Cubs once more.

I rushed back downtown to meet my family. "I've got this," I reassured my wife. "I've *got* this!"

The next night, the field announcer called my name and I tried to stride out to the mound with studied insouciance— whatever that is. I could hear 43,000 people in the stands— ignore me. The groundskeepers, who see this first-pitch show eighty-one times a year, went on raking; I think they only look up for hedgehogs and Bill Murray. My older daughter stood beside me and lowered the brim of her Cubs hat over her eyes. She would have deniability.

I turned around on the mound and looked toward home plate. Sixty feet and six inches away suddenly looked as far off as Paris. As the *moon*. I wound up in the imitation of Fergie Jenkins I remembered, and threw my pitch. It was low and outside but, thankfully, within the reach of a skilled professional bullpen catcher. I acknowledged the two or three cheers from the crowd with a Jeter-style doff of my cap. I still cherish the giggles of my daughter.

We rejoined my wife and younger daughter just as I was succeeded on the mound—by a Girl Scout. She was ten years old and wore pigtails under her Cubs cap. I think she had sold more Tagalongs than any other scout in Skokie. She was utterly adorable. She kicked up her left leg, cocked her arm, and threw a dead-solid perfect strike low over the plate. The crowd jumped to their feet and applauded until their hands stung. I heard cries of "Awwright!" and "Sign that kid!"

I went over to tell the mother of the skirted young Koufax, "You have a wonderful daughter." I lowered my Cubs cap over my eyes and slunk up to our seats. My dream would have to be revised. If the Cubs ran short of pitchers, the manager wouldn't say, "Where's the guy with the beautiful wife and cute kids?" He'd ask, "Where's the Girl Scout who throws like Clayton Kershaw?" And as a fan, I'd call out, "Over here!"

The 2014 Cubs were a last-place team. My flat, gasless pitch more or less melted without a ripple into a discouraging season.

But the Cubs were getting better. Tom Ricketts had competed to sign Theo Epstein, the general manager who had given the Boston Red Sox the right kiss on the lips to revive them from an eighty-six-year slumber, and won him with money, commitment, and the challenge to bring the Cubs out of suspended animation, too.

But Theo Ball is not the *Moneyball* of Billy Beane and the Oakland A's (who, by the way, have never won a World Series). A small-market team like the A's can give their fans one great year by working the system. The Ricketts family wanted to *own* the system. They gave Theo time and money to bring promising talent to their minor league teams, and build a development complex in the Dominican Republic. And when Joe Maddon, one of baseball's few original thinkers, had a loophole in his contract with the Tampa Bay Rays, the Cubs could pull out their big-market wallet and make Maddon the highest-paid manager in baseball.

"Why would you not want to accept this challenge?" he told reporters at a tavern. "In this city, in that ballpark, under these circumstances, with this talent, it's an extraordinary moment."

Joe Maddon seemed to look at baseball afresh through his horn-rimmed specs. He played with percentages by bringing in relief pitchers he'd shuttle to the outfield for an out or two so he could bring them back, or shifting the second baseman into right field for left-handed pull hitters, and he was once memorably tossed from a game for telling an umpire who commanded him not to utter another word, "I love you." Maddon brought the Cubs to a ninety-seven-win season in 2015, third best in baseball. But they were felled in four games straight in the first round of the playoffs by the New York Mets. The wipeout was humiliating. The Cubs had won all seven games against the Mets during the season. But they were defeated in the playoffs, not cursed, and learned that you don't get to carry over any credit from the regular season.

By 2016, the Cubs had developed, promoted, acquired, and traded for the elements of a team that had talent, but also a lot of character.

Jon Lester had gone through chemotherapy treatments for lymphoma when he was twenty-two, and came back the next year to pitch Boston into the World Series. The year after that, Theo Epstein brought a seventeen-year-old prospect Boston had signed into the clubhouse with his father because the kid had been diagnosed with cancer. Jon Lester talked to him a long time, but his advice boiled down to: *keep moving.*

Seventeen-year-old Anthony Rizzo would faint in the clubhouse that day. But he came to and pulled through. Epstein brought him to the Cubs, too. Rizzo was on the All-Star Team in 2014 and saw Jon Lester during warm-ups. "I don't know if you remember me . . ." Lester sure did. Rizzo told him that Chicago was a good place to play, and both men say they heard each other in a deeper way because of the harrowing circumstance that first brought them together. *Chicago is a good place to play.* Lester topped off a team where Kris Bryant was the reigning Rookie of the Year, Addison Russell and Javier Báez knit the infield tightly together, and Jake Arrieta looked like an Old Testament prophet throwing lightning bolts and no-hitters. My wife and I watched a game in May and she joked, "Darling, are we sure these are the Cubs?"

The Cubs ran out of more interesting people to ask and invited me to throw out a first pitch again in 2016. They'd gotten off to the best start in baseball: seventeen wins and just five losses. When I walked to the gym in my Cubs cap through the streets of New York, people no longer went, "Awww . . . ," as if beholding a gangly puppy, but started going, "Hey, Cubbies, *grrrhhh!*" In 2016, I couldn't just warm up in the park with an old pal and expect to make a pitch that would complement the new Cubs' prowess.

I asked my yoga instructor for help. Stephanie Sheridan

(whose website says, "Ignite Your Perfect Body," which would scarcely apply to me) was not a baseball fan. But she took a few days to study the pitch and met me at the gym one morning with a baseball.

"We'll wind up throwing it," Stephanie explained. "But first, we use it to roll out your psoas." The word sounds like *sore-ass*, but Stephanie pointed to a loin muscle. "That's where the pitch begins."

Pitchers have said that their delivery actually begins in the legs and hips. In recent years, more teams, including the Cubs, had worked yoga into training. So Stephanie had me roll the ball into my sore-ass—excuse me, *psoas*—for the setu bandha sarvangasana. Over the next few weeks, she had me lunge into the anjaneyasana and the virabhadrasana, and twist myself into the one-armed swastikasana. ("I know it's an old Hindu symbol," I told Stephanie. "Way before Nazis. But we have *got* to get another word for this pose.")

I could feel my psoas bulge with new power under my shorts (at least I think it was my psoas). "But how am I supposed to grip the ball with it?" I asked Stephanie.

"Your chakras will know," she told me. Those cunning bastards.

By the time I arrived at Wrigley, on the last day of July,

the Cubs had the best record in baseball. They were in first place in the National League Central Division, six and a half games ahead of the St. Louis Cardinals. Our daughters wore their Cubs hats with swagger.

Max Berman, entertainment coordinator of the Cubs (he is the grandson of the founders of a classic Chicago hot dog stand called Superdawg; in Chicago, this is like being the Prince of Wales) met our family and friends at the gate. "Just nice and easy over the plate," he told me, "and take a seat in the bullpen if we need you later."

Max had e-mailed me a few weeks earlier to ask what number I wanted to wear. After a few minutes of thought, I wrote back: 34. It was the number worn by the late Walter Payton of the Chicago Bears, who died, too young, from cancer, and suffered too much from injuries and anti-pain medications. It was the number worn by Kerry Wood, the Cub who struck out twenty in his fifth career start, then struggled gamely with arm trouble for the rest of his career. Number 34 had *history*.

The Cubs played the Seattle Mariners. Wrigley Field was bright and brimming, the setting sun painting a rosy glow on the grandstands. My heart brims, too, at Wrigley. I have a story for each section of the field and the seats:

My father and I were there . . . I'd meet Uncle Jack over

there . . . Santo would do his dance down that baseline . . . That seat: Steven Bartman . . . Ernie's five hundredth, just above the basket in left, hit the bottom row, hey-hey . . . Stu and Jimmy and I once sat up there . . . Uncle Charlie played there . . . Aunt Marian dribbled his ashes down that line . . . I wonder if they still have those great Polish sausages over there . . . The day after I graduated from eighth grade—no, wait, it was Sunday, two days later—we sat over there, against the Astros. Billy and I shouted, "Hey, Houston, what's it like to play baseball in an aquarium?" but they still won . . .

Games can be long nights for my family.

Max took us onto the field. We said hello to Wayne Messmer, the great voice and gentleman who sings the national anthem, and a couple of longtime ushers. "Geez, your daughters are getting big. This year has been great . . ." I heard my name. I strolled to the mound as if I'd been called in from the bullpen. The grounds crew kept on raking. Our older daughter held up an iPhone to send out video of my pitch, and I could see her grin behind the screen. I pretended to shake off a sign. I started my windup in my psoas, rocked back, turned, kicked out my left leg, twisted my hips, kicked back with my right leg, brought through my right shoulder, and let the ball leap from my fingers. I watched the red seams spin for a suspended moment, and heard about a dozen people cheer.

My throw might have been a strike on LeBron James.

The game turned out to be a milepost for 2016. Every fan has a different game to cite, but that night's 7–6 defeat of the Mariners signaled to many of us that the Cubs weren't just charmed: they were for real.

The Cubs fell behind 6–0 in the first few innings, while Seattle's starter, Félix Hernández, struck out eight and three Mariners hit two-run homers. Cubby bats whiffed through the air. But in the stands, fans turned to one another to say: *wait*. Joe Maddon brought in seven pitchers (I like to think I would have been the eighth). He sent five players to play left at various times, including Travis Wood, a relief pitcher, who snatched a long fly ball in the ivy vines, and Willson Contreras, a catcher, who dived in the grass for a sharp fly. I'll say he's a catcher!

Kris Bryant opened the ninth inning with a strikeout. But Anthony Rizzo doubled. Addison Russell singled to send him home. Willson Contreras turned what might have been a dribbler to begin a double play into an infield hit. Then a wild pitch opened home for Addison Russell to tie the score at the last possible moment, and the game went into extra innings.

Our younger daughter, who had been holding her head, eyes shut, against my wife's shoulder, sat up in all the claps and cheers. "Are they winning yet?"

As the clock on the scoreboard rotated toward midnight at the bottom of the twelfth inning, Jason Heyward hit a double and moved up to third. Joe Maddon called in Jon Lester, the pitcher, to pinch-hit.

Jon Lester is one of the best pitchers in baseball. But he walked to the plate with a .051 career batting average. Lester would have a slightly better mathematical chance of getting a base hit than he would of being bitten by a pink unicorn. Seattle pulled in their infielders, in expectation of a bunt. The first pitch from Cody Martin, the Mariners' pitcher, backed Jon away from the plate: ball one. Lester ran his hands down his bat to bunt the second pitch, but it was too high to get down; he took strike one. Jason Heyward hastened back to third. Martin then threw a pitch-out, so Mike Zunino, the catcher, could fix a glare on Heyward to hold him there with the cock of his throwing arm. Lester swung away at the next pitch. He nicked it just enough for a foul, strike two.

Jon Lester is not rattled—in fact, he is steely—in the stress of critical situations, which are exactly the plays that make a man's reputation. Lester came to Boston, he came to Chicago, and the World Series followed. I believe Jon Lester will be in the Hall of Fame. But Lester struggles with a mental block: he can't throw the ball to first base (I find this only an appealing frailty). Yet that night, with the winning run on his toes ninety feet from home and down to two strikes, Jon punched a short, solid, dead bird of a bunt that rolled to a stop about six feet from home plate, and a yard or so from the first base line.

The catcher, Mike Zunino, lunged forward to grab the ball in his bare hand and leaned back, practically yoga style, to reach for a tag on Jason Heyward's sliding toes before he could touch home plate. It was a great Seattle defensive play—and it missed by an inch.

Heyward didn't slide. He dove headfirst and did a controlled skid to the far side of the plate to reach over with his left hand and tap out the run that won the game in the bottom of the twelfth inning. It was a moment to love about baseball: two great plays by both teams, decided by an inch.

It was just before midnight, when the calendar would flip to August and Cubs fans worried about any lead wilting in the swelter. *But not this year.* White "W" flags flapped in the stands like birds taking off in a flock. Choruses of "Go, Cubs, Go" rolled through the stands. Pitchers and a catcher had snatched outs from hits in the vines and the grass, and a pitcher had pinch-hit the winning run home with a bunt in the dirt.

Down on the field, Jon Lester was hugged, mobbed, and clapped on the back as if he'd just run through rifle fire to deliver a keg of brandy. His teammate Cubbies doused Lester's smooth head with the contents of their water bottles, and it sopped his jersey until it was dark.

Jon Lester wore number 34. Another notch for history.

"You got guys all over the place doing different things that they're not used to and playing all over the map," Jon said later. "Joe [Maddon] does it again. You kind of sit there sometimes and scratch your head, and it seems to always kind of work out at the end. So it was good."

We got back late and dawdled over breakfast the next day. For the twentieth time—no, more like the thirtieth— I announced to my family, "Amazing, wasn't it? Utterly amazing." Our older daughter is thirteen, and not easily impressed. She just said, "Aw, I knew they'd win." That game would begin a thirteen-game winning streak for the Cubs that would extend their lead to twelve in the National League Central Division. It was the first day of August in the summer of 2016, and the Cubs and their fans were changing, as much as their team.

• • •

The Cubs played the Cleveland Indians in the 2016 World Series, and I wish it had been almost any other team. During a year of my childhood, my father was the field announcer for the Cleveland Indians. "Batting in the fourth position, number seven, the right fielder . . ."

It was the last year that my parents were married, and I went to the ballpark with my father for most game days. Lunch was a hot dog, and peanuts were the vegetable course. It was the finest summer of my childhood. I'd tag along with my father to receive the official lineup cards from each manager, and I got to look around for a few cherished moments to see boyhood idols in jockstraps and sweaty T-shirts.

Our family feels a connection to Cleveland. It has much of the character we love about Chicago, a city of hardworking people who have a wink in their eye. *Major League* (the original, not its sequels), in which fictional Cleveland Indians win the World Series, may not be as good a film as Bergman's *The Seventh Seal*. But which one do you want to watch again with a pizza on Saturday night?

Just about everything that can be said about the

prolonged drought for the Cubs winning the World Series can be said about the Indians, just for forty years less. We know what a World Series championship would mean to the city, and want nothing but the best for Cleveland. Just not against the Cubs.

My wife and I watched over dinner in a Chicago bar the night the series opened in Cleveland and the Cubs got Klubered. Corey Kluber, the Indians' superb right-handed pitcher, struck out eight batters in the first three innings, and by the fourth we didn't have much of a taste for anything. My wife turned to ask, "He can't pitch every game, can he?" No, just two or three. The Indians won that first game, 6–0. When I told her on the walk back for the night, "Well, darling, it's just one game," my wife reminded me, "That's what you always say. Game after game."

We watched the second game behind the stage at a literary awards dinner for the Chicago Public Library. All these years we've been going to these awards, and never a worry that there would be a postseason schedule conflict. Thankfully the award winners, Erik Larson and Scott Turow, weren't interested in coming onstage for acclaim until the Cubs were ahead, 5–1, which is how the game ended, the series tied.

We had to return to Washington, D.C., the next night

to see our friend and companion at Cubs games Rick Bayless, the triple-threat Chicago chef, restaurant owner, and cookbook author accept another award. It was an off night for the clubs to travel, or I'm not sure Rick himself would have made the trip. I caught his eye when one of the officials bestowing his award said, "This year, everyone is a Chicago Cubs fan," and I think we both winced. I wanted to rise and say, "Oh yeah? Everyone is a Cubs fan this year? This year is a *breeze*! You're not a Cubs fan until you've had your heart and hopes twisted into small pieces and eaten by a goat! You're not a Cubs fan until . . ." My wife kept a hand on my arm until she could be sure of me.

I came back to Chicago for game three. I felt it was a time for all of us who'd spilled love for the Cubs for so many years to come home, the way you would for a wedding, a funeral, or serious surgery on a loved one. You wanted to be there to celebrate. You knew you had to be there, too, if the worst happened, to grieve, swear, and help pick up the pieces.

I figured the Addison Street El stop would be swarming, so I decided to walk along Clark Street from the North Loop to Wrigley Field. Twenty blocks from the park, I was strolling through a sea of Cubby blue, people in Cubs caps, Cubs sweatshirts, Cubs scarves (Cubs socks, too; I had on a pair myself). The police shut down the streets for blocks around the park, and men and women walked over the white lines, laughed in the gutters, and clinked paper cups of beer as the sun sank softly over the west side of the city and striped Clark Street with strokes of gold. I passed a bakery that flew the four-starred flag of Chicago, the rainbow flag of gay equality, the tricolor flag of France—and the white, blue-lettered "Fly the W" flag.

I met my friends Marc and Maureen Schulman in front of the park. We could see the "W" flag run up from the win two nights ago in Cleveland. We hugged one another and just said, over and over, "Can you believe this? Can you believe this?" *The World Series at Wrigley Field.* It was like waking in a dream.

We met a young woman and her younger brother who had grown up four blocks from Wrigley. The woman lived in New York now. But she'd flown back to bring her little brother over to Wrigley, to breathe in the merriment and moment in the streets they knew from growing up around the ballpark. She said they'd watch the ballgame in a bar, sister, brother, and nachos. The brother turned out to be thirteen, the same age as our older daughter. Impulsively, I put my arms around the young man. "You will remember this for the rest of your life," I told him. I hope he knew—I think he did—that I meant he'd remember he had a sister who would fly home to bring him out to look up at the ballpark on an enchanted night.

Billy Williams, now seventy-eight, threw out the first pitch. Unfortunately, he couldn't bat, too. Cleveland won, 1–0, and when Javier Báez went down swinging for the last out of the third game, the tying and winning runs were on base. There weren't many fireworks in the game, but the Schulmans and I noticed that the click and flash of cell phones were like a field of lightning bugs in the stands. It was a World Series game at Wrigley Field. We Cubs fans were trying to burn it into our minds before it could melt away.

I walked to Wrigley the next night, too, and kept bumping into and falling into conversation with people who were on their way just to stand outside the ballpark and be close to something extraordinary.

But the Cubs got Klubered again, 7–2. I wound up sitting next to a Chicago alderman and his family. "Can't you do something about this?" I demanded. In the grand old days, Richard J. Daley would have installed one of his guys from the Board of Elections in the scoreboard so deceased Cubs could score runs, too, and make the totals CLE 7 CUBS 10. *Hey-hey, everybody, one last RBI for Ernie Banks!*

Walking back, I stopped at a nearby bar to call my wife,

who had watched the game with our daughters. There were a hundred people in the bar, wearing Cubby blue and speaking in subdued tones. But the mood was *not* funereal. The Cubs were down, three games to one, but the Cubs' extraordinary season, Bryant, Rizzo, Arrieta, Lester, Russell, and Báez, had the effect of green tea, vitamin B_{12}, and omega-3 fatty acids on Cubs fans. There's no mood enhancer like 103 wins. We didn't expect to win. But we also no longer assumed that some astral fate had ordained the Cubs must lose. My wife told me, "They'll just figure out some other way to win."

There was also a winning vignette in that bar: Vince Vaughn, the Chicago film star who sang "Take Me Out to the Ball Game" during the seventh-inning stretch, bought drinks for some of the policemen who worked security at Wrigley and had just gone off shift. He shook their hands and asked about their jobs and families. It was a nice reminder of the traits I treasure about the city. Chicagoans respect hard work and remember how to say thank you.

The fifth game was the next night, Sunday. The Indians were ahead, three games to one. It could be the last game of the 2016 World Series—that Cleveland won.

Or, the game that sent the series back to Cleveland. Whatever result, it would be the last game of the extraordinary year at Wrigley Field.

But on my way to the park, I stopped in my tracks. I had gone to two World Series games at Wrigley Field, and the Cubs lost them both. Any Cubs fan would have to wonder: What if I was the problem?

I didn't mind being in the ballpark if the Cubs were going to lose the World Series that night. In fact, I'd like to be there to help 45,000 of us give the Cubs a standing O and blubbering thanks for an unrivaled season. But if there was even of a wisp of a chance that my being in a seat at Wrigley was preposterously responsible for the Cubs losing, why risk those odds?

People were coming to Wrigley from all over North America to buy tickets on the street for thousands of dollars. Shouldn't I sell mine, fatten our daughters' college fund, and let the Cubs play this most critical game ever without worry that a fan in the stands would spoil their last chance?

I called my wife. She heard me through and pointed out that if I didn't go into the park and the Cubs won, I could never walk into Wrigley Field again. I could never watch them on-screen again. Could I even dare to check the score the morning after? I would have to stop being a Cubs fan. My devotion would be as dangerous to them as a kiss from a poison dart frog (I had to look that up). "Darling," my wife said, "you would never forgive yourself for not being there." Unspoken but understood was, *Do you think you have another 108 years to wait?*

It was a close, tense game that burned a lot of stomach acid and vigil candles. Jon Lester, adding luster to number 34, struck out the side in the first inning. In the second, Carlos Santana of the Indians hit a tall pop foul that came down near the camera well behind the first base side of home plate. David Ross, Lester's superb personal catcher, lost track of the ball in a puff of lake winds. The ball slipped out of Ross's bathroom sink of a catcher's mitt. But David's friend Anthony Rizzo had sprinted over right behind him. The ball sputtered, popped, and finally curled up in his first baseman's glove for an out: crisis averted.

Ross said he told Rizzo, "Hey, I'm just trying to make you look good."

But José Ramírez of the Indians followed. He's a versatile utility infielder who then displayed maximum utility when he hit a home run off Lester. It was 1–0, Indians, and Cubs fans had to contemplate that their team hadn't scored more than two runs since they'd come home to Wrigley Field. Take a Tums and light that candle!

Just an inning later, Trevor Bauer, the Indians' pitcher, chopped at a Lester pitch and sent it spinning high in the air along the right field foul line. It was a potential out as big, fat, and bright as the moon in the sky. The ball appeared to fall between the ledge of the wall and the Cubby-capped heads of the fans in the first-row seats. Have we seen this scene before? Jason Heyward, the right fielder, ran toward the brick wall in right, as Moisés Alou had run toward the wall in left in 2003. The fans in the first-row seats looked up and reached up with their hands, while thousands in the park looked at them. I heard people in the seats around me: "Ohhh nooo . . . Hands off . . ."

Heyward leapt to put his head above the wall and stuck out his left hand on top of the ledge to lift himself up for the ball. The fans saw his head and pulled back their hands. But the ball got caught in a gust of Lake Michigan wind, which took it back toward the field. Heyward adjusted valorously. He reached back with his gloved right hand, Bolshoi style, as he pushed himself back toward the field and caught the ball as his feet hit the field.

The crowd exhaled the ghost of a curse and cheered. A

woman sitting a couple of rows ahead of us said, "I had a cow." I didn't doubt her. I had stomach rumblings myself.

Trevor Bauer clapped his bat against his hand in tribute. It was a gracious gesture that went unreturned the next inning as Kris Bryant greeted Bauer with a solo home run. Anthony Rizzo lined the next pitch off the right field ivy for a double. Trevor Bauer threw three balls to Ben Zobrist, then came across with a fastball that Zobrist lined to left. Rizzo held up at third. Addison Russell tried a bunt, but it rolled foul. So he sliced a roller down the third base line and beat the throw to first. Anthony Rizzo galloped across with a run, and for the first time since the Battle of Hastings in 1066, it seemed, the Cubs took a lead, 2–1.

Jason Heyward, his defensive highlight secure, then struck out. Javier Báez laid down a beaut of a bunt to load the bases, and David Ross, in his last game ever at Wrigley Field (until he manages the Cubs one day—I predict this), hit a deep fly ball to left, and Ben Zobrist scored. The Cubs were ahead by two runs.

The Indians got the tying run to second base in the seventh inning. But then Joe Maddon called for Aroldis Chapman. They had brought him over from the Yankees three months before, amid much controversy. Chapman was the fastest pitcher in baseball. He could throw a ball that peaked at more than a hundred miles per hour, and had saved twenty of the twenty-one ball games in which he'd appeared for the Yankees. His pitching style had the flash and drama of a rocket blast (one of his nicknames: the Cuban Missile).

My wife and I had seen Chapman pitch earlier in the summer, when he had first joined the Cubs, and we remembered how a batter had barely gotten his bat in front of a fastball to thud a slow roller toward the mound. The hitter ran for first at full steam. Chapman reached down with slow, almost languorous ease to pick up the ball and throw it to Rizzo at first with the unhurried manner of a man playing catch with a child. The runner was out by just a few, teasing steps. My wife turned to me and said, "He's a star."

But Aroldis Chapman had also served a thirty-day suspension early in the season for violating baseball's domestic violence policy. He denied the charges, and none were filed. But he did admit to shooting a gun and said, "I did not in any way harm my girlfriend that evening. However, I should have exercised better judgment . . . ," which is not inspiring. Tom Ricketts and Theo Epstein talked to Chapman before bringing him to the Cubs, and insist he was more convincing. But it was not a player acquisition that seemed to fit the Cubs' character.

That night in Wrigley Field we saw Chapman take the mound with the game, the series, and the season at stake. He went to work, huge-shouldered, unhurried, and with a hundred-mile-per-hour fastball that got José Ramírez flailing like a man trying to hit a gnat with a bat in a windstorm. The crowd just went, "Oooh." Chapman was like the hired gun that the friendly little town on the prairie brings in for protection. You didn't have to like him. But you had to tip your hat in thanks.

Aroldis Chapman is a closer, the steel arm that strides to the mound for the ninth inning with his team ahead and hammers the last nails into the wooden overcoat (as we call coffins in Chicago). But someone who throws a ball at three-digit speed must be deployed sparingly.

He got a strikeout to open the eighth inning. Then Rajai Davis of the Indians hit a ground ball to first that drew Anthony Rizzo from the bag, and Chapman, who might find base runners to be unfamiliar foreign objects, failed to cover first. The fastest man on the field was now the tying run. Jason Kipnis followed. Chapman got him to hit a pop-up foul. Francisco Lindor came up next, and Chapman extravagantly ignored Davis on the base paths as he stole third. Thus undistracted, Chapman struck out Lindor with three swift strokes. He had already thrown thirty pitches, just two short of his season high, and had another three outs to go.

When the ninth inning opened, they came quickly: Mike Napoli grounded out, Carlos Santana flied out, and José Ramírez was left flat on his instep for the second time in the last three innings, and the last out of the night. The last play of the 2016 season at Wrigley Field. The Cubs had won by only a run, but just when they had to. In the end, that's what wins championships.

Drawn by my personal magnetism, the woman standing next to me in the grandstands threw her arms around my neck.

"Perhaps we should meet. I'm Scott."

"Wasn't that amazing! I'm Audrey."

Audrey introduced me to Seth, her boyfriend. "Didja see that?" he asked.

"I've been here all night."

"Yeah, but *didja see that?*" Seth repeated. Cubs fans had to turn to one another to be certain of what they'd just witnessed.

My wife called in the happy din, laughing. "Oh, darling," she said, "I knew you'd finally come through!"

None of us were in a hurry to leave Wrigley Field that night. Who knew if another century would ever bring us back? Choruses of "Go, Cubs, Go" broke out all over the grandstands and within a couple of stanzas mingled into one song. "Hey, Chicago, what do you say, the Cubs are gonna win today!" People rocked, swayed, teared up, clapped, chanted, and sang. Some of the players, heads still wet from a shower, stood on the dugout steps for a look, and then took a step up to the field to wave, shaking their wet heads and smiling. I found myself thinking of all the Cubs who never had a chance to step up into such adulation, and all the fathers, mothers, and grandparents for whom the Cubs had been a life's devotion that could crack our hearts, but renew our faith.

No team had come back from a 3-1 deficit to win the World Series since 1985. Only three teams had ever done it with the last two games on the road. But Kris Bryant, his hat turned around on his slick head, asked the post-game press conference, "Why not us? That's kind of how we do it. We play best with our backs to the wall."

I had some friends who asked if I'd like to go to Cleveland. But I had to get back to work and family, though I knew, like most fans, I would build my life around game six. I assume I addressed many important issues during the business day, and devoted myself to my wife and children. But the day passed in a blur until I heard the national anthem.

The Cubs won, 9–3. Jake Arrieta threw five strong innings. But the moments that would have been scrutinized and second-guessed until the Billy Goat closed came in the last three innings. Joe Maddon brought in Aroldis Chapman.

It was the seventh inning, and the Indians had a couple of runners on base. The Cubs needed to shut down a rally. Bringing in your flamethrower when you need critical outs, instead of just to close the game in the ninth when a lead is in hand, is the kind of original thinking that had twice made Joe Maddon Manager of the Year.

But the Cubs were ahead, 7–2. Chapman had thrown forty-two pitches in the fifth game, just two nights before, which is already half a game for most starting pitchers. Chapman stopped the rally cold (flamethrower and firefighter metaphors will begin to run into each other when you talk about a great relief pitcher). But the Cubs were about to play their biggest game since, well, 1908. Would their most imposing pitcher be at his best when they might need him most?

The seventh game of the 2016 World Series, which

would within a few hours be called one of the great World Series games of all time, began when the string section of the vaunted Cleveland Orchestra led 38,000 fans in an inspirational rendition of the national anthem.

Then Dexter Fowler hit Corey Kluber's fourth pitch over the center field wall. The ball bursting through the air gave proof through the night that the Cubs were still there.

Cleveland tied the game in the third when a Carlos Santana single brought home Coco Crisp, who had opened the inning with a double off of Kyle Hendricks. But the Cubs got back the lead in the fourth, as they began to finally solve Corey Kluber. Kris Bryant got a single. Anthony Rizzo was clipped by a pitch, but thrown out at second on a Ben Zobrist grounder that still sent Bryant to third. Addison Russell lifted a pop-up to center field and Kris Bryant slid just under Roberto Pérez's gloved tag at the plate. Willson Contreras stroked a Kluber curve into center that brought around Ben Zobrist to score.

The superb Kluber stayed on the mound until the fifth inning. Then Javy Báez opened the proceedings by hitting his pitch to right center, in the seats just above the Key-Bank key sign: 4–1, Cubs.

Then there was another highlight for millions watching. Fox Sports will turn a microphone and cameras on select players at certain times during a game to capture dramatic sounds and conversations. I am not a big fan of this dramatic form (no doubt Fox Sports would say the same about me). Most conversations go something like this:

PLAYER A: *They're hitting the ball pretty hard.*

PLAYER B: *Yup.*

PLAYER A: *Guess we just got to give a hundred and ten percent, huh?*

PLAYER B: *Yup.*

PLAYER A: *You said it!*

PLAYER B: *You bet!*

EXCITED ANNOUNCERS: *There you have it, straight from the field!*

I do not expect players to be sparkling conversationalists during a game (quite a few players can be cleverly profane and colorful, but know they shouldn't on Fox Sports, so they wind up sounding as staid as an NPR pledge drive). But the camera preserved a human moment between Anthony Rizzo and David Ross, the thirty-nine-year-old reserve catcher who had not yet been called into the game and was set to retire after the last out.

After Báez's home run, Rizzo walked over to David Ross, who watched from the front of the dugout with his arms folded over a railing. Rizzo put an arm over his friend's shoulder. "I can't control myself right now," said Rizzo. "I'm trying my best."

"It's understandably so, buddy," Ross told him.

"I'm emotional."

"I hear ya."

"I'm an emotional wreck."

"Well, it's only going to get worse," David Ross told the man who was a dozen years younger and a breakout star— but anxious. "Just continue to breathe. That's all you can do, buddy. It's only gonna get worse."

"I'm in a glass case of emotion right now," Rizzo told him.

David Ross was direct, unsparing, and practical with his friend.

"Wait until the ninth with this three-run lead."

It was a moment to remind us how young the men are we watch so closely, and how they're expected to excel under unfathomable attention. Rizzo peeled himself open in front of forty million people in the most pressurized moment of his life. Or was it? Maybe cancer survivors like Anthony Rizzo don't have to show they can be hard-boiled.

David Ross, for his part, didn't try to mollify his friend, but gave it to him straight: "It's only gonna get worse." But you can get stronger. It is one of the great moments of a great World Series, and it happened between plays.

The Indians brought in Andrew Miller, their most strapping pitcher. He throws a slider that would make fighter pilots cringe. But you still have to get it over the plate. Kris Bryant dueled Miller to a walk. Anthony Rizzo, breathing just fine now, golfed a single to right, and Bryant, who ran on the pitch, scrambled all the way around to score. The Cubs had five runs on the board through five innings.

Joe Maddon brought in Jon Lester as Cleveland opened their half of the fifth. This meant bringing in David Ross, too.

No one catches Lester like Ross. He knows his pitches, and tries to protect him against having to throw pickoffs or make plays at first, where the revered hurler has a disarming mental block. So when Jason Kipnis sliced a ball that dribbled to the left of the plate, Ross leapt on it and threw to first. But his throw flew wide, which left runners at second and third ("I must have been aiming for the crapper," Ross said later on ESPN). Then Lester let slip a pitch that skipped into the dirt. The ball jumped and bopped David on the chin of his mask. The unexpected jolt seemed to knock him on his backside. The catcher gamely twisted himself around to go after the ball. It rolled away, as balls do. Two runs scored, including Kipnis, who slid under Jon Lester's tag at home plate. It was 5–3, and the Indians were suddenly behind by just two runs.

"I get in the game five minutes," Ross said, "and give up two runs. They bring me in to stop runs."

Then David Ross came up in the sixth inning and hit a long fly ball into the deepest avenue of center field that just cleared the fence in front of a stand of trees. Cubs fans, who love David Ross, made even a little more room in their hearts. The last at-bat of his career was in the seventh game of the World Series, against one of the toughest, flintiest, sneakiest, and stingiest pitchers in baseball, and he hit a home run. It was 6–3, Cubs. A fan could begin to wonder if the curse of the Cubs has been banished by such notes of grace.

Ross's battery-mate, Jon Lester, got two quick outs to open the Cleveland half of the eighth inning. But José Ramírez stroked a ball through the middle that Addison

Russell couldn't quite grasp. And then Joe Maddon brought in Aroldis Chapman. He would need to get four outs to win the World Series for the Cubs. Did Chapman still have enough wick to burn?

Chapman's first pitches topped a hundred miles per hour. But his aim was off as he strained for speed. Brandon Guyer, a journeyman outfielder mostly famed for getting to first by getting hit by pitched baseballs (his nickname: "La Piñata") finally hit the ball with his bat instead of his elbow and drove it for a double that scored a run. It was 6–4, Cubs, but Cleveland was closing fast. Then Rajai Davis came up, choked up on his bat, and punched a fading Chapman fastball into the first row of seats just above the left field wall. The seventh game of the World Series was tied. And Chicago's most fearsome pitcher was running out of gas.

Cleveland fans bopped, danced, and hugged strangers in their seats. LeBron James and J. R. Smith of the world champion Cleveland Cavaliers whooped and yelped from their skybox. But the many Cubs fans who had made the trip from Chicago held their hands to their heads and shook them out, as if they'd just seen a dirigible disappear in the air. Something great was gone in a flash. Chapman looked merely human. He pulled his jersey over his face to wipe his eyes and nose. When he finally reached the dug-out after striking out Yan Gomes to end the inning at last, he seemed to blink tears.

Jason Heyward got on first on a fielder's choice to open the ninth inning, stole second, and advanced to third on a bad throw. But the Cubs couldn't score him. Chapman showed steel coming back to the mound to shut down the side, and the seventh game of the World Series would go into extra innings. Cubs fans were fearful—no other word fits—that the old curse their team had discredited all year long was about to take revenge.

Then the rains came.

It was a storm front, bright blue—almost Cubby blue on television radar—that swept in from the west across Lake Erie (the west, and *Chicago*). Umpires announced a rain delay. Grounds crews, feet slipping and sloshing, pushed huge rolls of white tarpaulin swiftly across the field. My wife and I told our daughters that they had to get to bed. The rain delay could last for ten minutes, or two hours. They were stretched out on the floor, fighting sleep to a draw.

"Wake me up," said our thirteen-year-old, "when something happens." I told myself that if the Cubs lost, I'd let her sleep, and hope to skip a new generation of children who have night terrors about the Cubs.

Tom Ricketts, the Cubs' principal owner, was sitting in a box seat alongside Cleveland fans and told himself he should get down to the dugout.

"Not to give any speeches," he said, but to tell his manager he believed in his team and was grateful for their extraordinary year. "What happens happens." But the crowd was so thick, and the rain so heavy, Tom and his wife went up to the club's suite, out of the storm, and by the time they had picked their way through all the people, the rain delay was over, after just seventeen minutes.

"The team took care of things," said Mr. Ricketts.

The Cubs filed out of their dugout and into the visitor's locker room, looking weighed down and dispirited. They looked like the Cubs of fabled and dubious curses, not the team that won 103 games.

No one recalls anyone saying, "Listen up." But the players (no coaches, executives, or Joe Maddon, they say) faced one another in a circle. Jason Heyward began to speak. He'd had a disappointing first year on his $184 million contract, superb in the field but hitting just .230 with seven home runs, the lowest numbers of his career. But

Heyward is a strong man, and a sturdy teammate. Quietly, he paid for David Ross to have hotel suites when the Cubs traveled so the friend he found so valuable could bring along his young family to share his last year in baseball.

Accounts of what he said are pretty consistent. Heyward began by saying, "I want you to remember how good you are. How good *we* are. I am proud of us—every single one of us. Every man on this team has played a part in getting us here. Kris [Bryant], with his great year. Albert [Almora], in his first year, Miggy [Miguel Montero], whenever he's needed. David, always coming through. We have everything we need to win. We just have to believe in each other and play for each other. We're the best team in baseball for a reason. Play our game, look out for one another. These are your *brothers*. Fight for your brothers. Lift them up. Stay positive. We've been winners all year. Let's go out there and be *us*."

I have a dream; the only thing we have to fear is fear itself; we will fight them on the infield, we will fight them in the outfield, we will never surrender; go out there and be us. MLK, FDR, Winston Churchill, and Jason Heyward.

The rains blew over and the Cubs ran back onto a field that looked refreshed by a mist. Heyward's words still rang. Then the Cubs' Kyle Schwarber hit a Bryan Shaw fastball through the second base side of the field to get on base. Albert Almora came in to run for him. Kris Bryant lifted a fly to center, and Almora came back to tag the base and race to second.

The Indians chose to give an intentional walk to Rizzo, for good reasons. First base was open; a ground ball could begin a double play to end the inning. Ben Zobrist was next, and hit a grounder, as desired. But the Indians had on their shift for a left-handed hitter, and Ben's hit bounded down the third base line and scampered like a hare over the grass out to the Cleveland Clinic sign along the left field wall. Almora scored. Rizzo raced to third. Zobrist steamed into second. The Cubs had a one-run lead.

Bryan Shaw then gave an intentional walk to Addison Russell, with the same invincible logic: fill the bases, go for a double play. This time it was Miguel Montero who grounded a pitch into left field for a single that sent Rizzo home and gave Chicago an 8–6 lead going into Cleveland's half of the tenth inning.

I do not believe in curses. But I give thanks for blessings, like rainstorms that blow in from the lake just when the Cubs need one most.

. . .

Tom Ricketts once told us about the speech he delivered to minor league players in the Cubs' organization during spring training.

"You may not believe this," he said he told them, "but someday, the Chicago Cubs will win the World Series. And when they do, the men on that field in Cubs uniforms will not be ballplayers. They will be legends."

My wife and I felt shivers.

A few days after the Chicago Cubs won the World Series for the first time in 108 years, I asked Mr. Ricketts if he knew of any players who heard his speech as minor leaguers and were on the field when the Cubs fulfilled his prediction. Tom looked to his press rep in the conference room, who shrugged, then back at me and lifted his hands.

"They probably wouldn't remember it anyway," he said. "I'm not that good a speaker. I used to really rip that in *español*, too, for the Dominican guys."

We met in a conference room of his financial offices, which overlook a couple of the iron-muscled bridges that lace together Chicago's West Loop. I wore a suit and tie to meet with the chairman and principal owner of the

Chicago Cubs and chief executive officer of Incapital LLC. The chairman wore a plaid shirt and khakis.

The World Series trophy Tom Ricketts and his family brought home from Cleveland was making a round of appearances in the city. Wrigley Field didn't have what almost any junior high school in the country did: a trophy case. What for?

Tom Ricketts said with a smile, "After all, we're the Cubs."

He recalled the moment in Cleveland when Rajai Davis hit the bullet off Aroldis Chapman for the two-run home run that tied the World Series.

"You tell yourself, well, we're a good young team. If things don't break our way this time there'll be other times. But then you remember just how hard it is to get to that final series, and then how hard it is to get to that final game, those final outs, and wonder how many chances you get. You play good teams, but you have to be healthy. You have to be hot. How many chances do you get?"

Shortly after the game, Tom saw the artwork *The New York Times* had prepared to run if the Cubs lost. It was an altered version of Norman Rockwell's *The Dugout*, only this time with Joe Maddon's face looking mournful in Charlie Grimm's spot, Kris Bryant, Jake Arrieta, and Kyle

Schwarber wincing alongside him on the bench, and Tribe fans Tom Hanks and LeBron James blowing raspberries in the stands. Javier Báez's face was on the chagrined batboy.

"Which I thought was condescending to Javy," said Mr. Ricketts. "You know, it just reminds you that until you win, until you get that ring, until you get that trophy, no matter how many games you win, that image is still there."

Mr. Ricketts met his wife, Cecelia, in the bleachers of Wrigley Field. Tom and his brothers, Pete and Todd, and his sister, Laura, were college students in Chicago, from the prominent Omaha family of Joe Ricketts, the founder of the TD Ameritrade brokerage, and his wife, Marlene.

Tom and his siblings all lived in Wrigleyville. "Saturday and Sunday we were just bleacher bums," he says. "We always sat in the first row of center field. You could just send someone down and they could hand beers up. That was our strategy. You've got to have a strategy."

Cecelia was a med student, taking in the game with friends, and Tom Ricketts was struck by her wit and smarts. "Here's this fourth-year med student, out drinking beer in the bleachers on a Sunday afternoon. She's pretty cool. We just started talking," Tom says, "and now we have five kids." Dr. Ricketts is a practicing dermatologist.

Perhaps because the Rickettses were from Omaha,

Wrigley Field was a destination for them, Emerald City with baseball, not the dwelling spot of lovable losers. Thirty years later, when Tom had made his own mint in financial services, the Tribune Company advertised that the Cubs were available for sale. Tom thought it would be a fitting challenge for his family to help bring a World Series to Chicago. But Joe, the founding father, was a hard sell about investing in an enterprise in which there were thirty teams, but just one winner a year.

Tom took his father to a game on one of the rooftops overlooking Wrigley. His father told him that a baseball club didn't seem to be a solid investment. Tom swept a hand over the stands and surroundings. There were many more fans than seats.

"They sell three million tickets a year, whether they win or lose," Tom Ricketts told his father, who mused for a moment and then replied, "Oh. Well, this *is* a business." Tom then took his brothers and sister back to the Wrigley they remembered from their student days. The park sparkled. The neighborhood was packed with people laughing, cheering, and spending. Beer appeared. To own the team was a chance they could expect to open just once in a lifetime. Tom says Pete, Todd, and Laura just looked at one another and said, "Okay, we've got to try to do this."

When the Rickettses bought the Cubs in 2009, it restored family ownership. The Tribune Company was a publicly held corporation that had to show annual results.

"You did what you could for this year to get your season ticket holders to renew," said Mr. Ricketts. "To get your sponsors to renew, to keep your TV ratings up. We hit the pause button on that. I wanted to buy time for Theo [Epstein] to build a foundation and put together a team for the long view that will last."

(I have twice been introduced to Theo Epstein, president of baseball operations for the Cubs. I doubt he remembers either time. Theo Epstein will be in the baseball Hall of Fame and one day write his own extraordinary history of how he won the World Series with the Red Sox and then the Cubs. I can't think of any other human being who has given as many people as much pleasure, and I'm not forgetting J. K. Rowling, Jerry Lewis, or Vātsyāyana, the Hindu philosopher who wrote the *Kama Sutra*.)

Tom Ricketts went on:

"Theo used to tease me that we had a total role reversal. I'm supposed to be the impatient owner, and he's supposed to be begging for more time. It's the other way around. 'Dude, it's all right,' I'd tell him. 'Just do it the right way. I promise you.'"

"It's a tribute to the fans, really," Mr. Ricketts adds. "I don't know if other teams can truly do it quite like we did. But when you have fans who are so committed, and not only love the team but love the ballpark, we just kind of feel like as long as we were honest and just told them it's going to take a couple of years, everybody would stay in the boat. People did."

I was at a forum in Chicago with Tom Ricketts and Michael Lewis, the author of *Moneyball* and other bestsellers, in the fall of 2013. The Cubs had just finished in fifth place in the National League Central Division, thirty-one games behind the St. Louis Cardinals.

"Mr. Ricketts," I told him on the stage, "I hope the year is not far off when you will have a schedule conflict in October."

But Michael Lewis wondered if the Cubs had any incentive to improve. The Cubs took in a reported $266 million in revenue in 2013. They were one of the most profitable of all major league franchises—as a fifth-place team.

"Why would you want to get better, with numbers like those?" Michael asked.

But maybe even hugely successful authors like Michael Lewis just don't deal in the same kind of numbers as

Tom Ricketts. "I don't know anyone that takes big, big checks out of their team," he explains. If you repeat a championship—perhaps the hardest feat in team sports—it just costs you more money to achieve the same result, which is not a sound business plan.

"Now, between the day you bought the team, and the day you sold the team, you could have a lot of value appreciation," says Mr. Ricketts. His family bought the team for $700 million in 2009. Forbes now values the Cubs at $2.5 billion. But Tom Ricketts says his family wants to own the Cubs like the Wrigleys did, "for the long term, decades," and hopes the Ricketts children of the next generation will want to put their talents into the team.

This current generation of Rickettses has also gotten attention with political involvements all around the spectrum.

"We have a little bit of mix in the family, which to me is normal," says Tom. "I don't know why this surprises reporters. Is that so unusual?"

Joe and Marlene Ricketts are Republicans who supported Donald Trump, but only after trying to fuel Governor Scott Walker's campaign for president. Tom's brother Pete is the Republican governor of Nebraska. Their sister, Laura, is founder of a gay rights political action committee, and was a major Obama and Clinton contributor. She is the first openly gay co-owner of a major league team, and is already a member of the Hall of Fame—the Chicago Gay and Lesbian Hall of Fame.

Todd Ricketts is Trump's choice to be deputy secretary of commerce. But in 2016, after Scott Walker's campaign ran aground, Todd was one of the major forces behind Our Principles PAC, which sought to stop Trump from winning the nomination. Joe and Marlene joined him, and helped fund commercials that condemned some of Trump's crudest remarks.

"I hear the Ricketts family, who own the Chicago Cubs, are secretly spending $'s against me," Trump tweeted during spring training in March 2016. "They better be careful, they have a lot to hide!" Then he told the *Washington Post* editorial board, "I'll start spending on them. I'll start taking ads telling them all what a rotten job they're doing with the Chicago Cubs."

A month later, the Cubs would begin their season with seventeen wins and five losses for the best record in baseball, which they would keep the entire year. Some rotten job.

"It's a little surreal when Donald Trump threatens your mom," Tom Ricketts told me. "The fact is, whether it's my mom or my dad, or my sister on marriage equality, or my brothers on what they do, or what we do with the team, we're pretty much an open book. We stand up for what we believe in. That's what America should be. That's who we are."

Todd Ricketts and his parents wound up supporting Donald Trump. (And Theo Epstein prominently supported Hillary Clinton.)

"There are a lot of interesting conversations in the family," Tom Ricketts told me just before Thanksgiving. "I'm sort of in the middle. I don't think it's anything out of the ordinary. We all love each other. We all hang out together. Everybody has a good time with it."

Almost a more sensitive topic for Cubs fans is if Tom Ricketts has tried to restore relations with any of the names that figure into the folklore of team curses. He says the team has had occasional contact with people who know Steve Bartman. But Bartman prefers no attention; the Cubs will honor that. And Tom says he's never talked to any member of the Sianis family. "I've been to the Billy Goat for food, of course," he says. "I've never talked to them, the family, at all."

Tom Ricketts is the only person I've ever met who's gone to the Billy Goat for the food.

"But let me put you on the spot a little more," I asked

the morning we got together. "Joe Maddon. Great manager." Tom nodded. "But did he misuse Aroldis Chapman? Use him too much in game six?"

"Joe is a great manager," Tom Ricketts said simply. "Playoffs are different. Guys take different risks. There's just a different way that managers manage in that situation. He used his best judgment. We won, so we'll go with it.

"Baseball is different in so many ways," Tom added. "There are other sports that are a little flashier. But baseball is America's pastime. There's nothing even close in terms of how much time people spend with baseball. Day after day, for seven, eight months of the year. It is just part of your family. Taking the bus down Addison for our parade, I saw a little girl, maybe three or four, holding a handmade sign: 'We did it, Grandpa.' I'm sure Grandpa is no longer with them. But the Cubs are a love they share."

And the parade of five or six million people, who filled sidewalks, stood in streets, and packed into parks? Tom Ricketts leaned forward, and for the first time, his voice was a little thick.

"I don't know how to describe it. The number of people, the energy of the whole city on those streets. Driving home from the parade, all my kids were in the car. Suddenly it was quiet and everything was calming down and then I got a little weepy. *Wow: it really happened.* I knew it was a well-loved team. I met tens of thousands of Cubs fans over the course of the last seven years. But then to see just how big the parade was and how many people came and signed the names of loved ones who are now gone on the chalk wall.

"The Sunday after we won, there was like ten thousand people standing around the park, just hoping to get a glimpse of a guy walking out with a box of dirty clothes from his locker. I saw Justin Grimm. He said, 'I just came to pick up some dirty clothes and sneakers and people are cheering me down the street.'"

Tom Ricketts shook his head and looked out toward the river. "It's just . . . just . . ." He took a full stop before he could say, "Overwhelming."

It wasn't until later in the day, after I'd spent the morning with Tom Ricketts, that the Cubs announced they'd raise their season ticket prices an average of 19.5 percent. This is often a cue for commentators to fume against big-time sports and millionaire stars.

I just can't work up outrage. Wrigley Field still has ten thousand fewer seats than, say, Yankee Stadium. But fans from across the country make pilgrimages to Wrigley. Demand drives up prices. The Cubs, like most any major league club, sell discount seats under a variety of programs, including to groups, schools, clubs, honor roll students, hospital patients, and seniors. That should make it possible for most people to see a little baseball every year.

The 2016 season ticket holders who sold their seats to a ticket service for resale, even for just a game, easily doubled whatever they paid. And World Series games? Their profits were colossal. All of that money goes to ticket brokers and their bots, not the team fans go to see. The cost of a seat at Wrigley Field will be somewhere between a first-run movie and a stage play. That seems reasonable. If a team can't raise ticket prices after they win the World Series for the first time in 108 years, when can they?

But Tom Ricketts knows that the Cubs will no longer be cherished for how much they've suffered and endured. They'll be measured by wins, losses, and championships, not the charm of daytime ball and ivy on the wall. The Cubs have won the World Series. They're one of the most successful franchises in sports. They're a national brand. They need no introduction on *Saturday Night Live.* The Cubs are *expected* to win now, like Apple, ExxonMobil, and Meryl Streep.

But they came within just a few strokes of one more fabled failure in the last innings of the seventh game. If they had lost, talk of curses would have returned. The Rockwell portrait of forlorn faces in the dugout would be repainted. Sports pundits would trumpet that they knew Chapman would tire, and Heyward wouldn't hit. They'd bray that Joe Maddon was a genial, bespectacled soul who can get a young club into the World Series, but not the brash ass-kicker they need to win it. As Tom Ricketts said, nothing less than winning the ring would make history.

The Cubs now have what might be the hardest challenge in team sports: to win again. Twenty-nine other teams have spent months studying the Cubs and plotting how to beat them. They have players who will twist a knee on a slide, tear a muscle on a throw, or slip in the shower—or get clipped by a car, or overdose on a drug. Life intervenes. Some of the Cubs' best players (and best executives) will leave for more money, for greater fame, or to spend more time with their family. Every Cub from 2016 is part of a legend now; other clubs will offer them fat contracts just to wear their uniform and hope they've been touched with a winning spirit that will catch on in their club.

I didn't even have to polish the question for Tom Ricketts.

"Look," he said, "people ask me all the time, now, and even before, 'Do you think if the Cubs win, it will kind of somehow change who the Cubs are?' Well, I'm willing to find out. We'll take our chances. I think the Cubs will just grow. We've had this fan base, all these millions of people, giving all this love to this one team for all these years. They deserve more than one championship. So let's just keep it rolling."

There is one matter about which the Cubs are not eager to speak but worry will get worse. Will their 2016 World Series win inspire more people to find ways to scatter the ashes of their loved ones in the Friendly Confines?

It is not permitted. "No exceptions," says a team spokesperson.

Well, I know of a couple. When Charlie Grimm died at the age of eighty-five in 1983, my Auntie Marian told the Cubs that Phil Wrigley had promised Charlie his ashes would be sown into the soil along the first base line.

Marian said Cubs executives were aghast. If we let people sprinkle their departed loved ones in Wrigley Field, they said, the infield would be awash in ashes. Players would be spooked and choke on the embers of former fans. It's against federal workplace rules!

Marian went to the top. So in the late morning on a raw day in March, while the Cubs were at spring training in Arizona and grounds and maintenance crews worked to ready Wrigley Field, Auntie Marian and a few friends and family gathered in some of the green seats along the first base line. Club personnel shook hands all around and said, "Keep this to yourself, now. This is only for Charlie." A priest was present in a windbreaker. Our small group told him, "Bless all the Cubs bats while you're here!" Marian sang a few lines that seemed utterly perfect:

I'll be seeing you
In all the old familiar places . . . .

First base was an old familiar place for Charlie Grimm. Cubs staff brought Marian over to the first base soil. White baselines wouldn't be drawn into the dirt for a few more days, and the soil looked brick red. Marian held a blue box in her arms.

"Here we go, baby doll," we could hear her say, and she overturned about a cup of ashes into the area that would soon hold first base. A groundskeeper raked the ash gently. Marian put a kiss on the tips of her fingers and blew it into the dirt. She came back to the seats, where we all embraced her, and just said, "Well, how 'bout that, sports fans. Drink?"

It was not hard to find a bar open at 11:00 a.m. in Wrigleyville. And to this day, if our family sees a player hit the dirt around first base we say, "He gets a pocketful of Uncle Charlie."

Charlie Grimm's interment was officially sanctioned, if officially secret. But over the years, most Cubs fans have heard scores of unofficial sagas. People pack the ash of loved ones into baggies or old pill bottles, mutter a prayer during "Take Me Out to the Ball Game," and shake out cinders under a seat. North side cremationists report they often hear bereaved people say, "We're gonna sneak some of this into Wrigley, and let Uncle Ray go when the Cardinals are in town!" Cremationists cover their ears. "Don't tell me! You can't do that! But lots of people do!"

Steve Goodman, the great Chicago singer whose "Go, Cubs, Go" became so well-known in 2016, died of leukemia in 1984. He was just thirty-six, an artist, a joker, and a Cubs fan. We used to attend the same religious assembly, where we spoke little of spiritual concerns, but a lot about the Cubs (come to think of it, that's a lot about spiritual concerns). Steve's 1983 "A Dying Cubs Fan's Last Request" is a droll, lovely blues ballad in which a mortally ill fan asks for a Cubby funeral pyre at Wrigley's home plate.

*Build a big fire on home plate out of your Louisville
  Sluggers baseball bats,
And toss my coffin in
Let my ashes blow in a beautiful snow
From the prevailing 30-mile-an-hour southwest wind*

Steve died just a year later, shortly before he was to sing the national anthem at Wrigley Field. A while later, a couple of family members used the Chicago Way (a twenty-dollar bill inside a rolled-up *Playboy*) to convince a groundskeeper to unlock a gate so they could make a quick sprinkle of some of Steve's ashes in left field. Today, if an opposing player is slow to spring on a Cubs single to left, and Bryant or Rizzo takes an extra base, I like to think it's because Steve got under the left fielder's foot.

All fans look at playing fields and see the shadows of favorite players past. I think Cubs fans can look out at Wrigley and no longer see just demons plotting debacles, but think they see the spirits of their loved ones, dancing over the grass and dirt.

. . .

I can't write this praise of the Chicago Cubs world championship season without the sorrow of having to note that 2016 will also be remembered as one of the worst for murder in Chicago's history. At least 762 people were murdered over the year. More than 4,000 Chicagoans were shot. More people were shot to death in Chicago in 2016 than in New York and Los Angeles combined. It is a blight, a crime, and a disgrace for the city we love.

The disgrace also divides the city. Most homicides have occurred in just a few neighborhoods. They're not along Lake Shore Drive, the marble-faced towers of the Gold Coast, or, for that matter, the urban hipster districts around Wrigley Field.

Just eight of Chicago's seventy-seven neighborhoods, according to *The Trace*, a nonprofit news site about gun violence, have more than ninety murders every year for every hundred thousand people. These city blocks are names in the news every week: Englewood, North Lawndale, Washington Park, Grand Crossing, Fuller Park, and a few more. They are overwhelmingly on the south and west sides, in communities of African-American citizens, churches, and businesses.

But eleven neighborhoods have little more or even less than one murder per hundred thousand people. They include Lake View, Lincoln Park, and Edgewater, which are within a stroll of Wrigley Field (there is no neighborhood the city officially designates as Wrigleyville). These neighborhoods are *not* all-white. In fact, they are some of the most truly diverse in America, with blacks, whites, Hispanics, Asians, and Native Americans, and enclaves in which English is a second language to Polish, Spanish, Mandarin, Hindi, or Bosnian. The murder rate looks different on the north side of town. But people must know it is only good luck.

I am sickened by Chicago's homicide crisis, and appalled by attempts to politicize it. Donald Trump has tried to brandish Chicago's murders as proof of ineffective Democratic rule, in President Obama's own neighborhood. *The Trace* points out there are more homicides per capita in New Orleans, Detroit, Washington, D.C., and twenty other cities. Yet apologists and ideologues who try to dismiss outrage over the murder rate as a racist ploy to embarrass black leadership also dismay me. Each of the hundreds murdered was a person whose loss sends out ripples of grief and fear all across the city we cherish.

I have reported a lot of Chicago crime stories over the

years, from governors going to jail to street gangs ruling by blood and terror. I am under no illusion that tightening federal gun laws will cause gangs to line up like Boy Scouts to toss their Glock .40s and assault rifles into a police bonfire. I covered the war in Bosnia, where the UN earnestly imposed an arms embargo. I have begun to see similarities between guns and drugs: they are so powerful that people will pay dearly and risk everything to get them. I don't pretend to know what would stop this spilling of blood, tears, and the city's future, but I find it hard to see the Second Amendment's "right of the people to keep and bear Arms" upheld by the mayhem we see on Chicago's streets.

Five to six million people lined the blocks from Wrigley Field down to Michigan Avenue for the parade to welcome the Chicago Cubs and their World Series trophy. Six people in that crowd were arrested, mostly for being drunken jerks. Putting an end to Chicago's daily and nightly suffering would be a real championship to celebrate.

When Rajai Davis hit that home run in the ninth inning of the seventh game of the World Series, Anita Decker Breckenridge, deputy chief of staff for operations of the White House, was watching in a hotel room in Miami, where she had accompanied President Obama on a campaign trip.

Her phone rang. It was the man White House staffers call POTUS.

"I'm worried about you," said the president of the United States. "Come up here and watch the game with us."

Anita Decker had grown up in the northern suburbs of Chicago. Cody Keenan, the president's chief speechwriter, spent his early years in the Lakeview neighborhood on the north side. When the Cubs came to the White House for the last scheduled event of the Obama administration on January 16, 2017, the president strode into the East Room and began, "Here is something none of my predecessors ever got a chance to say: welcome to the White House the World Series Champion Chicago Cubs!"

A couple hundred of us sat on slightly squeaky gold ballroom chairs on the Fontainebleau parquetry floor laid down in the time of Theodore Roosevelt (who, as it happens, was president the last time the Cubs won the World Series; his children roller-skated over that floor), and below Gilbert Stuart's portrait of George Washington. The father of his country is shown holding out his right arm and raising his thumb. I like to think he was flashing the bunt sign to Jon Lester.

It was terrific to see the mayor of Chicago, senators from Illinois, state officials, Congresspeople, and cabinet members light up to see Cubs infielders, pitchers, and outfielders. Fergie Jenkins, Ryne Sandberg, Billy Williams, and José Cardenal were among the old Cubs seated in the great, gilded room, and little boys and girls in BRYANT, RIZZO, and BAEZ jerseys crawled over the laps of their influential parents and grandparents.

I sat alongside my friends the Schulmans, who had baked their Eli's Chicago cheesecakes for both of the president's inaugurals. They employed a lot of people from refugee families in their north side bakery, and Marc and Maureen often remind me: anyone can make the world a little better. You can do it making cheesecake. We'd watched a lot of games at Wrigley Field with the Schulmans, and I told them in the East Room, "Our best seats yet."

President Obama acknowledged that really, he's a White Sox fan. The White Sox last won the World Series in 2005, and Sox fans can get eloquently angry that the *dawing widdle Cubbies wooze* so much and still usually outdraw the serious team on the other side of town. But the Obamas have a mixed marriage. Michelle Obama used to watch Cubs games with her father, Fraser Robinson, when she got home from school in the afternoon. She greeted the players in the residence and told them how precious it had been for her to share the Cubs with her father.

"That's how people feel about this organization," said the president. "That it's been passed on generation after generation, and it's more than sports. And that is not just true for FLOTUS," he said. "My longest-serving aide, Anita, is a Cubs fan. When they won, the next day she said, 'This is the best day of my life.' And I said, 'What about me winning the presidency? What about your wedding day?'" We laughed in the squeaky seats. "She's like, 'No, this is the best.' My chief speechwriter, Cody Keenan," the president continued. "Cubs fan. In fact, there were a lot of sick days during the playoffs."

Boisterous laughs rolled out from White House staff members just in front of President Obama. The ballplayers and the staffers both had to play their best game under keen pressure and constant testing. But twenty years from now, many of the staffers will be senators, senior partners, or mayors. The ballplayers, for all the millions they make now, may find middle age their biggest challenge.

Cody Keenan and Anita Decker Breckenridge brought me back to Cody's office in the West Wing. He had packed up a lot as he prepared to leave the White House in just three days, but his Cubs caps and World Series tickets were displayed on a desk. I saw no photos of Cody with political figures, at conventions, or shaking hands with Hollywood stars.

"This is one of my top five days here," said the president's chief speechwriter. He tried to recall the others. "Getting Bin Laden. Passing the ACA. Marriage equality . . ." We should perhaps not mention whatever other major policy initiatives fall behind the Cubs coming to the White House.

I told them that, aside from Chicago loyalties, I was surprised the Cubs made such a quick trip to the White House. Presidential welcomes were usually set after the next season opened. Had Donald Trump's tweet "I hear the Ricketts family, who own the Chicago Cubs, are secretly spending $'s against me. They better be careful, they have a lot to hide!" made the family loath to be congratulated by President Trump?

Anita Breckinridge shook her head. "I was with the president when he called Joe Maddon," she said, and showed me a photo. "He told him, 'Look, I'm a White Sox fan, but a lot of north siders are on my staff, and it would mean a lot to them if you came to the White House.'"

I was embarrassed to have looked for political intrigue in what might have been simple kindness.

I told Cody Keenan I had been especially moved by the remarks the president made toward his close, when he remembered the Cubs' welcome-home parade: "Millions of people, the largest gathering of Americans that I know of, in Chicago. And for a moment, our hometown becomes the very definition of joy."

The copy of the speech from which the president read was on Cody's desk. He flipped it to the final page.

"That was something POTUS just said on his own," he said, and pointed to the last paragraphs. "See? It's not in there. We'll add it to the transcript later."

What President Obama said, in among the last remarks of his administration, was "Sometimes people wonder, well, why are you spending time on sports, there's other stuff going on . . . Throughout our history, sports has had this power to bring us together, even when the country is divided. Sports has changed attitudes and culture in ways that seem subtle but that ultimately made us think differently about ourselves and who we were. It is a game and it is celebration, but there's a direct line between Jackie Robinson and me standing here. There's a direct line between people loving Ernie Banks, and then the city being able to come together and work together in one spirit."

I told the president's chief speechwriter, "I think it's the greatest presidential address since Gettysburg."

The Chicago Cubs came out for the last half of the tenth and their best chance to win their first World Series in 108 years with Carl Edwards Jr. on the mound. He was twenty-five, ostrich-skinny, and wore his cap slightly off-kilter, as if he'd just put it back on in the wind. Carl struck out Mike Napoli. He got José Ramírez to ground out to Addison Russell. But then Carl walked Brandon Guyer on just five pitches. The Cubs' defense pulled back to play for just one last out, and let Guyer steal second without a challenge. But Rajai Davis was up, and he delivered again, this time with a single that scored Guyer.

The Cubs' lead dwindled to a single run. The run that could tie the game danced off of first base. I hoped—I think I even prayed—for rain to return.

Joe Maddon brought in Mike Montgomery to pitch to Michael Martínez, a career .197 hitter. He clipped a slow ground ball toward shortstop. Kris Bryant didn't want to wait. He leapt forward from third to grab the ball in his glove and stood up to fire across the infield to first. The grass was wet and his legs slipped from under him. His throw was a little high.

Kris Bryant could have fallen on his face. His throw could have been another inch higher, rolled toward the stands, and brought in Rajai Davis. A century of disastrous possibilities played at lightning speed in the minds of Cubs fans in that second. But Anthony Rizzo went up on his toes. He brought down the ball with Martínez three solid steps from first base, and stuffed it in his back pocket. A cry of a century went up.

I gripped my wife's arm. My eyes filled. I sputtered, as I had in so many dreams, "I can't believe it! I can't believe it! . . ." as so many Cubs and loves past and present piled all over the mound, for once not only in my mind, but in a sea of Cubby blue.

My feeling for the Cubs is love, not loyalty. It has not always been pure pleasure to be a Cubs fan, but it's never been a chore, and, overwhelmingly, it's been fun.

You begin with Wrigley Field, a fountain of brick and ivy under the El tracks, as much a neighborhood fixture as a school or house of worship, a place that stays rooted year after year even as businesses, restaurants, family trees, and the languages that play through the streets change. Then there are those storied teams, with their varied characters, including the luminous Ernie Banks, jolly Charlie Grimm, the sturdy Billy Williams, Bill Faul, a pitcher who hypnotized himself (but couldn't hypnotize batters), Carmen Fanzone, a true utility fielder who played baseball by day and the trumpet in clubs up and down Lincoln Avenue at night (he went on to play, a little more productively, for the Baja Marimba Band); and today's Cubs, with the racehorse grace of Kris Bryant, the bluff charm of Anthony Rizzo, the John Brown beard and fiery eye of Jake Arrieta, the interlocking elegance of Russell and Báez at short and second, the bullet-headed and brawny-armed Jon Lester, and the flinch he must overcome each time to get the ball to first; and the sweep of the Cubs' story over a century, losing, pulling close, falling down, coming back, looking forward, just going on, day after day.

So we beat on, to borrow from Fitzgerald, *batting against current pitching, hoping not to be borne back ceaselessly into the past.*

The Cubs have been a love I have shared with my father and my grandfather, my wife and my daughters, and sometimes a language to connect us when words might only drive us apart. I am suspicious about trying to draw lessons from the love of a sports team. But loving the Cubs has taught a lot of us, not just Cubs fans, that life is more about trying than winning; and trying again; and then *again*.

Our daughters have heard that history. But they are growing up with Cubs who win the World Series, go to the White House, make their father cry for joy, the president smile, and turn out what may be the largest crowd to ever see a parade. People still tell our daughters that they're cute when they wear their Cubs hats, but they go *Grrr* instead of *Awww*.

I think that's wonderful. A parent wants something better for his children.

I sat for a long time after the Cubs won and watched every drop of champagne douse them in the locker room. I saw every interview, listened to every scrap of postgame analysis, and watched every replay, beer commercial, and ad for erectile dysfunction pills. It took hours before I could be sure it wasn't just a dream.

I thought of my father watching the Cubs, when they were all he had to hold in his heart on long afternoons, and the two of us (row 13, seats 15 and 16) sitting and talking between pitches. I thought of Uncle Jack and uttered,

"Hey-hey! Hey-hey!" over and over. I remembered my mother's lilt of a laugh when Charlie Grimm would say something outrageous, and how tickled Charlie would be to see base runners slap his ashes—I can hear Charlie roar this—off of their asses. When I said a long "Hey-hey!" aloud one more time before bed, it was softly, almost like *Amen*.

I stepped into the bedroom of our older daughter. I slipped my arms around her. I told her gently, "Baby, the Cubs won. They *won*," and she opened her eyes just enough to find me and smile back. "Awww," she said, "I knew they would," and fell back to sleep as I held her and looked out at the winking lights of a boat that drifted slowly over the river outside our window.

ACKNOWLEDGMENTS

I owe thanks to many people for help on this book: Aileen Boyle, David Rosenthal, Gwyneth Stansfield, and Katie Zaborsky at Blue Rider Press/Penguin Random House; Max Berman, Dennis Culloton, Mike Grossman, Tom Ricketts, and the Chicago Cubs organization; and the many friends who made crucial contributions: Deann and Rick Bayless, Drs. Edward Benzel and Neil Cherian of Cleveland Clinic (who confirmed that my blood is Cubby Blue), Mike Flannery, Rhona Frazin, Lewis Karp, Clive Richardson, and Marc, Maureen, and Kori Schulman.

And the incomparable Kathy Layne.

I am grateful to Sarah Lucy Oliver for her understanding and support in this and so much more. And to Wayne Kabak for more than I can say.

And thanks to the 2016 Chicago Cubs for an unforgettable year. Come to think of it, even the 107 years before that were unforgettable.

All mistakes are mine alone.

And always to Caroline, Elise, and Paulina (and now Daisy). They are my loves, and my life.

ABOUT THE AUTHOR

Scott Simon hosts *Weekend Edition* Saturday mornings on NPR, heard by more than four million people every week. He has reported from all fifty states and six continents and covered ten wars. He is also a contributor to *CBS Sunday Morning* and is the author of eight books that range from the bestselling memoir *Unforgettable: A Son, a Mother, and the Lessons of a Lifetime*; the novels *Pretty Birds* and *Windy City*; and *Just Getting Started*, a memoir with Tony Bennett. Simon has won every major award in broadcasting and received the State of Illinois Order of Lincoln in 2016. He is married to Caroline Richard Simon, and they have two daughters, Elise and Paulina.